HOLY TERROR

HOLY
TERROR

Terry Eagleton

OXFORD
UNIVERSITY PRESS

OXFORD

UNIVERSITY PRESS

Great Clarendon Street, Oxford OX2 6DP

Oxford University Press is a department of the University of Oxford.
It furthers the University's objective of excellence in research, scholarship,
and education by publishing worldwide in

Oxford New York

Auckland Cape Town Dar es Salaam Hong Kong Karachi
Kuala Lumpur Madrid Melbourne Mexico City Nairobi
New Delhi Shanghai Taipei Toronto

With offices in

Argentina Austria Brazil Chile Czech Republic France Greece
Guatemala Hungary Italy Japan Poland Portugal Singapore
South Korea Switzerland Thailand Turkey Ukraine Vietnam

Oxford is a registered trade mark of Oxford University Press
in the UK and in certain other countries

Published in the United States
by Oxford University Press Inc., New York

© Terry Eagleton

The moral rights of the author have been asserted
Database right Oxford University Press (maker)

First published 2005

All rights reserved. No part of this publication may be reproduced,
stored in a retrieval system, or transmitted, in any form or by any means,
without the prior permission in writing of Oxford University Press,
or as expressly permitted by law, or under terms agreed with the appropriate
reprographics rights organizations. Enquiries concerning reproduction
outside the scope of the above should be sent to the Rights Department,
Oxford University Press, at the address above

You must not circulate this book in any other binding or cover
and you must impose this same condition on any acquirer

British Library Cataloguing in Publication Data

Data available

Library of Congress Cataloging in Publication Data

Data available

Typeset by RefineCatch Limited, Bungay, Suffolk
Printed in Great Britain
on acid-free paper by
Clays Ltd., St. Ives plc, Suffolk

ISBN 0–19–928717–1 978–0–19–928717–8

1 3 5 7 9 10 8 6 4 2

To Alice,
with apologies for the world
we have brought you into

Preface

This book is not intended as an addition to the mounting pile of political studies of terrorism. Instead, it tries to set the idea of terror in what I hope is a rather more original context, one which might loosely be termed 'metaphysical'. As such, it belongs to the metaphysical or theological turn (or full circle) which my work seems to have taken in recent years, one welcomed by some but looked upon with alarm or exasperation by others.[1] As far as the exasperation goes, I would point out to my friends on the left that the politics implicit in this rather exotic talk of Satan and Dionysus, scapegoats and demons, are more, not less radical than much that is to be found in the more orthodox discourses of leftism today.

In any case, terrorism itself is not political in any conventional sense of the term, and as such poses a challenge to the left's habitual modes of thought. The left is at home with imperial power and guerrilla warfare, but embarrassed on the whole by the thought of death, evil, sacrifice, or the sublime. Yet these and allied notions, I believe, are quite as germane to the ideology of terror as more mundane or material conceptions. Like a number of my recent books, then, this one seeks to extend the language of the left as well as to challenge that of the right. Perhaps this is partly because I live in a country which used to teach politics and metaphysics together in its national university, and in which it has not been unknown for hairdressers and bus drivers to have a passing acquaintance with notions of natural law or theories of just warfare.

The genealogy I trace for terrorism, all the way from ancient rites and medieval theology to the eighteenth-century sublime and the Freudian unconscious, may look not only arbitrary but perversely unhistorical. It is the former in the sense that it is not, of course, the only pre-history of the phenomenon that could be sketched; it is the latter, I think, only in a somewhat impoverished understanding of the historical.

Some of the material in the book was delivered in different form as the Sir D. Owen Evans Lectures at the University College of Wales, Aberystwyth in 2003, and as the Alexander Lectures at the University of Toronto in 2004. I am deeply grateful to my hosts in both establishments for their kindness and hospitality. As always, I am also greatly indebted to the wisdom and friendship of my editor Andrew McNeillie.

T.E.

Dublin
2005

Contents

1

Invitation to an Orgy

LIKE many a supposedly antique phenomenon, terrorism is in fact a modern invention. As a political idea, it first emerged with the French Revolution—which is to say, in effect, that terrorism and the modern democratic state were twinned at birth. In the era of Danton and Robespierre, terrorism began life as state terrorism. It was a violence visited by the state on its enemies, not a strike against sovereignty by its faceless foes.

The word 'terrorist' emerges in the context of such French Revolutionary terms as 'Girondist', and it is suggestive, if unhistorical, to read it as a satirical send-up of them. The *ist* suggests, sardonically, a sort of philosophy—but one which comes down to spilling guts and hacking off heads, and thus a wholly bankrupt kind of theory. To be called a terrorist, then, is to be accused of being cleaned out of ideas, conjuring a grandiloquent doctrine instead out of the simple act of butchery. It is rather like calling someone a copulationist, implying that their high-sounding notions are just a fancy cover for fornication. The word may be intended to make you sound pretentious as well as sinister. As such, it is dangerously misleading. Terrorists, whether of the Jacobin or modern-day variety, whether Islamic fundamentalists, Pentagon promoters of shock and awe, or conspiracy theorists huddled in the hills of Dakota, are not in general bereft of ideas, however malign or preposterous their ideas may be. Their terror is intended to help execute their political visions, not substitute for them. And there is a complex philosophy of political terror in nineteenth- and twentieth-century Europe, which can by no means be reduced to simple thuggery. The word 'terrorist' is an underestimation.

In a broader sense of the word, to be sure, terrorism is as old as humanity itself. Human beings have been flaying and butchering one another since the dawn of time. Even in a more specialized sense of the term, terrorism runs all the way back to the pre-modern world. For it is there that the concept of the sacred first sees the light of day; and the idea of terror, implausibly enough, is closely bound up with this ambiguous notion. It is ambiguous because the word *sacer* can mean either blessed or cursed, holy or reviled; and there are kinds of terror in ancient civilization which are both creative and destructive, life-giving and death-dealing. The sacred is dangerous, to be kept in a cage rather than a glass case. The idea belongs to a reflection on the enigma of the linguistic animal: how come that its life-yielding and death-dealing powers spring from the same source, which is to say from language? What is this self-thwarting animal which ends up being persecuted by its own creative powers?

The affinity between terror and the sacred may sound peculiarly, even offensively irrelevant to the terrorism of our own time. There is nothing especially saintly about tearing someone's head from their shoulders in the name of Allah the All-Merciful, or burning Arab children to death in the cause of democracy. Yet it is not wholly possible to understand the notion of terror without also grasping this curious double-edgedness. Terror begins as a religious idea, as indeed much terrorism still is today; and religion is all about deeply ambivalent powers which both enrapture and annihilate.

One of the earliest terrorist ringleaders was the god Dionysus. Dionysus is the god of wine, song, ecstasy, theatre, fertility, excess, and inspiration, qualities which most of us are likely to find more endearing than estranging. Most of us would prefer a spree with Dionysus to a seminar with Apollo. Protean, playful, diffuse, erotic, deviant, hedonistic, transgressive, sexually ambiguous, marginal, and anti-linear, this Bacchic divinity could almost be a postmodern invention. Yet he is also an unbearable horror, and for much the same reasons. If he is the god of wine, milk, and honey, he is also the god of blood. Like an excess of alcohol, he warms the blood to chilling effect. He is brutal, rapacious, and monolithically hostile to difference—and all this quite inseparably from his more alluring aspects.[1] If he has the charm of spontaneity, he also betrays its mindless ferocity. What makes for bliss also makes for butchery. To dissolve the ego ecstatically into Nature, as Dionysus does, is to fall prey to an atrocious violence. If there can be no unflawed happiness with the ego, neither can there be any without it.

The god's bewitched camp followers, who throw plundered human organs to the winds and tear men and women limb from limb in their crazed rapture, can be seen as thrillingly emancipated from the dull regime of reason; but they can also be seen as the doped captives of a quasi-fascistic cult. They represent a vital collective or Dionysian democracy, but one which in disowning hierarchies is mercilessly intolerant to anyone who steps out of line. For the Bacchic women who worship the god, as for some modern-day purveyors of cultural junk, those who criticize their way of life are elitists out of touch with the unreflective wisdom of the folk, and thus to be vilified. Dionysus himself is a shameless populist whose appeals to custom and instinct are among other things a smack at the impiousness of intellectual critique. It is a familiar authoritarianism of intuition. Like any number of despots and dogmatists, the followers of Dionysus simply consult their hearts.

If Dionysus has all the fathomless vitality of the unconscious, then, he also has its implacable malevolence and aggression. He is the god of what Slavoj Žižek, after Jacques Lacan, has called 'obscene enjoyment' or horrific *jouissance*.[2] His heart-warming, spine-chilling liturgy is a version of Hegel's so-called Night of the World—that orgy of un-meaning, before the dawn of subjectivity itself, in which bloody stumps and mangled bits of bodies whirl in some frightful dance of death. It is a dark parody of carnival—a jubilant merging and exchange of bodies which like carnival itself is never far from the graveyard. The orgy dissolves distinctions between bodies, and thus prefigures the indifferent levelling of death. Indeed, in the terms of Freud's *Beyond the Pleasure Principle* this god of ease and self-gratification represents a pure culture of the death drive—of the merciless imperative which commands us to reap joy from our own dismemberment. Dionysus is the patron saint of life-in-death, a connoisseur of the kind of energy we reap through reckless self-abandonment. The vitality he offers his disciples has the hectic flush of death about it. In his mysterious rites, self-affirmation and self-dissolution are interwoven.

Dionysus is part bestial and part divine, and to this extent a pure image of humanity—of the oxymoronic creature which is always either more or less than itself, either lacking or excessive. Both gods and beasts are lawless—the latter because they fall below the law in their amoral innocence, the former because in dispensing the law they are considered to be set above it. They can demonstrate their freedom from the law by putting it in suspension, which in a different way is what the criminal does too. Indeed, the lawgiver has much in common with the law-breaker, as Hegel points out. History for Hegel is forged by a succession of mighty legislators who are forced to transgress the moral frontiers of their time simply because they are in the van of progress. Raskolnikov proposes much the same view in Dostoevsky's *Crime and Punishment*. In the eyes of modernity, the criminal and the avant-gardist, or the outlaw and the artist, are closely allied.

Almost nothing in Freud's writing—certainly not the idea of infantile sexuality—is as offensive to common sense, as likely to leave the mind as outraged and incredulous, as the scandalous proposal that men and women unconsciously desire their own demise. Yet literature is littered from end to end with illustrations of our being, in Keatsian phrase, half in love with easeful death, one of the most moving of which is to be found in Thomas Mann's novel *Buddenbrooks*. As his life draws to a close, Thomas Buddenbrook recognizes in a precious epiphany that 'death was a joy, so great, so deep that it could be dreamed of only in moments of revelation like the present. It was the return from an unspeakably painful wandering, the correction of a grave mistake, the loosening of chains, the opening of doors—it put right again a lamentable mischance' (Part 10, ch. 5). In Freud's terms, it is life or Eros which is the painful wandering undertaken by the ego in its hunt for the bliss of extinction. The problem, as we shall see, is to distinguish between the kind of love of death which is really just a raging appetite for annihilation, and the view that only by paying our dues to death as the ultimate signifier of our frailty and mortality can value accrue to the living. It is the latter mode of existence which Hegel has in mind when he remarks in *The Phenomenology of Spirit* that though death is of all things the most dreadful, 'the life of the Spirit is not the life that shrinks from death and keeps itself untouched by devastation, but rather the life that endures it and maintains itself within it'.[3]

It is this acknowledgement that Pentheus, ruler of Thebes in Euripides's play *The Bacchae*, disastrously refuses to make. Confronted with this blow-in deity Dionysus and his marauding troupe of female revellers, the arrogant Pentheus reacts with a violence grotesque enough to match Dionysus's own. With blasphemous impiety, he threatens to cut the god's head from his shoulders, smash his sanctuary with crowbars and topple it to the ground. (We shall see later that another ancient Greek sovereign, the Theseus of Sophocles's *Oedipus at Colonus*, reacts in quite a different manner when confronted with another ambiguously holy and defiled creature in the figure of Oedipus.) Reason, faced with libidinal riot, goes berserk, as one kind of excess (anarchy) provokes another (autocracy) into being. Pentheus, one might venture, reacts to the cult of Dionysus rather as the FBI reacted to the cultists at Waco.

It is not immediately apparent, then, who exactly is the terrorist here, as Dionysus, god of licence, calls sharply upon the king to control himself. As one commentator remarks, 'Pentheus and his enemy are fighting on the same terms and in the same spirit.'[4] This lord of misrule is even temperate enough to offer to negotiate with his opponent, a compromise which the high-handed Pentheus contemptuously spurns. As with human civilization itself, Dionysus's rationality and self-discipline are entirely genuine, not mere paper-thin masks or rationalizations of an underlying fury. It is no surprise that this avatar of Thanatos or the death drive suggests a bargain—for that drive, so Freud argues, is always ready to choose a circuitous path to its desired goal, a path which is nothing less than what we know as life.

In rebuffing the god's diplomatic overtures, the king of Thebes shows himself up as a pharisaical prig, a man whose panic-stricken reaction to cultural otherness is 'Clap it in chains'. This pig-headedness catalyses violence rather than constrains it. Pentheus is an exponent of state terrorism, ready to mobilize an entire army against a band of unarmed women. He is an ethnocentric bigot, who on being informed that the cult of Dionysus is common in the East, sniffs 'No doubt. Their moral standards fall far below ours.'[5] This 'womanish' stranger Dionysus and his crew hail from the Orient, which is a large part of what Pentheus finds so unnerving about them. Yet though this god is a stranger to the city, he is already ensconced covertly in its heart, and certainly lurks deep somewhere in its outraged sovereign. The trouble with Dionysus is that he is both outlandish and intimate. In fact, this is probably how he would have struck Euripides's original audience, who would no doubt have got wind of this flamboyant foreign deity, but who might also have found him as exotic as Pentheus does.

At once morally smug and hair-raisingly reckless, the autocratic Pentheus is as much a fanatic in his own way as Dionysus, and to this extent an allegory of our own political times. (There are, to be sure, a few telling differences from some of our own political leaders: the Chorus, for example, calls Pentheus 'eloquent' as well as obstinate.) Euripides's Chorus insists in the face of Pentheus's bull-headedness that violence is not what governs human affairs, meaning perhaps that there is no enduring social order which does not rest on consent. Even the exercise of force must be backed in the end by general agreement. If you greet the violence of others simply with red-necked repression, you are likely to have your buildings blown to pieces, as Pentheus's palace is shattered by Dionysus, while crazed religious zealots (the Bacchic women) tear you to pieces and dabble elbow-deep in your blood in a grisly parody of the eucharist. The hunted become the hunters, and the victims the masters. Like Oedipus, Pentheus believes himself to be the pursuer only to discover that he has become the prey. King and criminal, lawmaker and lawbreaker, are hard to tell apart.

For Euripides's great drama, it is not a matter of approving of Dionysus, but of giving him his due. This is what the recurrent word 'reverence' signifies in the play. Reverence, in effect, is the opposite of repression—of that self-blinded form of sovereignty which cannot bring itself to recognize the disruptive, double-edged nature of the forces which give birth to civilization, and which sustain it in being. Of these, the most obviously double-edged is sexuality, which quite literally produces the social order but which is always potentially anarchic in its excess. There is more to sexuality than social reproduction, and it is that dangerous supplement which threatens to disrupt the scrupulously regulated orders of kinship. An example of this is incest, motif of so much tragic drama from Oedipus onwards. The act of incest illicitly conflates places in the symbolic order which ought to remain separate; but for that order to operate, such places must be in any case combinable and interchangeable. Incest is thus a deviation which must always be possible if sexual norms are to be upheld. It is simply a more dramatic illustration of the inherent plasticity of common-or-garden desire. In its interweaving of the alien and the intimate, it also has relevance of another kind to Euripides's play.

What helps to found political society, then, also figures as the enemy within. The power which plays its part in bringing responsible citizens into existence also threatens to shatter them as human subjects. If desire cuts across jealously calibrated civic hierarchies,[6] it does so not just because it is agreeably egalitarian but because, like despotism, it is no respecter of persons. The trouble with sexuality, as comedy is aware, is that it is has no regard for rank, since anyone can desire anybody else. Social hierarchies stem from a source which is ruthlessly indiscriminate. In its cavalier way with distinctions, Eros has much in common with its old antagonist Thanatos. It is our own terrible powers, then, which we are invited to approach with fear and trembling, so that reverence becomes the reverse of a complacent self-love. It means an openness to that at the core of the human which remains alien and opaque to it. In this sense, the gods, who are signs of this inscrutability, pose a potent challenge to the more narcissistic kinds of humanism.

The callowly rationalistic Pentheus cannot see that reason, to be effective, must be rooted in forces which are not reasonable in themselves. To censure his rationalism is thus to secure the sway of reason, not to write it off in the name of some modish celebration of the senses. We are not being invited in the manner of some left-bank café liberationist to opt for Dionysian orgy against bloodless rationality, but to realize that no form of rule or reason can flourish which does not pay its respects to the elements of unreason which lie at its heart. As Hans Castorp, another of Thomas Mann's protagonists, reflects in *The Magic Mountain*: it is love, not reason, which is stronger than death, and from that alone can come the sweetness of civilization— 'but always in silent recognition of the blood-sacrifice' (ch. 6). At the centre of Hans's utopian vision in the snow is the ritual dismembering of a child.

The sweetness of love, then, must pay its dues to what Mann

in *Death in Venice* calls the 'monstrous sweetness' of death. But unreason is not simply a question of violence and monstrosity; it is also, as Mann sees, a matter of love, which is neither reducible to rationality nor independent of it. It is only when reason is nurtured by the 'unreason' of love that it has the power to confront that more malign form of unreason which is the lust for destruction. Otherwise, thrown back on its own feeble resources, it will prove powerless to stem this annihilating force. This is why rationalism and nihilism are cronies as well as rivals, as we shall see later in the case of D. H. Lawrence's *Women in Love*.

This is why Freud is among those philosophers who deconstruct the age-old opposition between reason and passion. Reason can restrain our disruptive desires only by drawing its own energies from them, fuelling itself from this turbulent source. If it is not in itself passionately *engagé*—if it lacks the force and bodiliness of desire—it will simply end up as a version of Pentheus's anaemic pragmatism. The critic William Empson no doubt had something like this in mind when he remarked that 'the most refined desires are inherent in the plainest, and would be false if they weren't'.[7] A reason which has no anchor in the senses,[8] like a sovereignty which simply rides roughshod over its opponents, will become like Pentheus a prey to the very forces against which it struggles. Being too aloof from those powers, it will fail to shape and inform them from within, and so will allow them to run riot. This is one of several reasons why the authoritarian preserves a secret compact with the anarchist.

This is what happens to yet another of Mann's fictional heroes, the austerely self-disciplined Aschenbach of *Death in Venice*. Aschenbach seeks an Apollinian, formally perfect art only to find himself in the grip of a Dionysian lust for death, disease, and negativity. This is partly because nothing is more perfect than nothingness: for the symbolist poet, the purest work of art is as unblemished as the void itself, free from the base contaminations of matter, and so both everything and nothing. There can be no sense without language, yet the manhandled stuff of discourse can only corrupt such meaning. But it is also because the more reason dissociates itself from its base in the sensuous body, the less it can mould the senses from the inside, and so the more unruly and obstreperous they become. The more you sublimate life into translucent form, the more of a prey you become to deathly dissolution. Once again, formalism and nihilism, autocracy and anarchy, turn out to be sides of the same coin. The Apollinian and the Dionysian are not such strangers to each other after all, as Pentheus discovers to his cost. As the play unfolds, he shifts from icy legality to illicit desire, no longer the scourge of the Bacchic cult but its helpless dupe. Finally he will be led forth, clothed as a woman, to his doom. Angelo, the thin-blooded autocrat of Shakespeare's *Measure for Measure*, is another city governor who discovers that a law founded on the repression of desire simply strengthens its sway over you.

In *Beyond the Pleasure Principle*, Freud observes something of the same contradiction at work in civilization itself. The more men and women sublimate Eros or libido into the task of building a culture, the more they deplete its resources, thus leaving it disarmed in the face of its old antagonist, Thanatos or the death drive. There is something curiously self-thwarting for Freud about the whole business of making history. It is dependent upon powers which are perpetually capable of sinking it without trace. These powers—Nature, sexuality, aggressivity, and the like—are not meaningful in themselves, any more than the marks which make up a language have inherent sense. They are, rather, the material infrastructure of meaning, the senseless foundation of our sense-making.

Culture both draws upon and represses these potentially anarchic powers; indeed, without some degree of blindness to them, it could not survive. Repression is essential to our exist-ence. Oblivion is more fundamental to us than remembrance.

With Pentheus and his crew, however, the unavoidably injurious business of repression is pressed too far and becomes a form of sickness. Reason at its extreme limit capsizes into madness, becoming a mirror-image of the very savagery it seeks to quell. 'I am sane and you are mad', Dionysus coolly informs the incredulous king. It is sane to acknowledge madness, and lunatic to imagine that such madness could ever simply be bullied into reason. Reason on its outer edge is demented because it seeks to possess the whole world, and to do so must override the recalcitrance of reality, the way in which it kicks back inconveniently at reason's own paranoid projects. But to deny the substance of the world's body in this way is to be deranged. The wielder of absolute power is a fantasist, for whom reality has the endless pliability of desire. The most materialist of civilizations is in this sense idealist to its core. There can be no absolute power without a world on which to exercise it, but there can be none with such a world either. Without resistance, power ceases to be present to itself and suffers an inward collapse; with resistance, it can no longer dream of its own perfection.

If civilization and barbarism are near neighbours as well as sworn antagonists, it is partly because the evolution of humanity brings with it more sophisticated techniques of savagery. We are not more rapacious than the Etruscans, merely supplied with sleeker technologies of domination. But it is also because culture cannot thrive without a degree of subjugation of Nature. Those sentimentalists who regard such a project as always and every-where reprehensible should ask themselves whether they would care to set up home on the ocean bed, or be infected by one loathsome virus after another. Human cultures are dredged from the chaos of Nature, and without the organized violence which this involves, there would be no eco-warriors around to regret the fact.

For the later Freud, this drive to subjugate our surroundings is a version of Thanatos or the death drive. Instead of directing that lethal violence upon ourselves, we turn it outwards, and in this way escape being torn apart by it. In deflecting this perilous power outwards, we press it into the service of humanity by harnessing it to the ends of Eros, builder of cities. Yet Thanatos is a fickle, duplicitous servant who is secretly in revolt, forever slipping free from the civilizing project and scampering off to do his own thing. In the forging of civilizations, the death drive is harnessed to soberly functional ends, growing strategic and astute; but it continues to betray a delight in power and destruction for their own sake, which continually threatens to undermine those ends. What this implies, then, is that the urge to order is itself latently anarchic. The enterprise of constructing civilization is infiltrated from the outset by death. What makes for human culture also mars it. The very force which is intended to subdue chaos is secretly in love with it.

This means that the drive to regulate Nature is madly in excess of necessity. There is something pathological about this rage for order: it conceals a ferocious inner compulsion which is the very opposite of freedom. Fundamentalism is one symptom of this disease. In the name of a desire for absolute security, cities are shattered, blameless civilians burnt and dismembered, and whole generations turned rancorous and resentful. One thinks of Shakespeare's Macbeth, who undoes his regal power in the very process of trying to render it impregnable ('To be thus is nothing, | But to be safely thus'), and who thus dies in a sense of ontological anxiety. We are dealing here with a desire which provokes the very turbulence it seeks to quell. Security means fending off the frightful disorder which death represents. Yet death itself is the only ultimate sanctuary, which is why those lusting after total security find it so secretly attractive. Nothing is less assailable than nothing. Death is the reverse of raucous and unruly, which is why it is the fantasy of the police officer and bureaucrat as well as of the nihilist. It is not in fact true that the dead cause no trouble: the dead cause us an infinite amount of trouble. But it is an understandable illusion. In the domain of ideas, this deathly perfectedness is known as fundamentalist dogma.

Dionysus is beyond the pleasure principle, inhabiting a realm of lethal ecstasy. He is thus not the other of Pentheus but a possibility which lurks unsettlingly within him, the expelled and disavowed kernel of his own selfhood. There is that at the heart of human civilization which is profoundly antithetical to it. A certain 'terrorism' is built into our preciously wrought civility. Without a dash of barbarism, no civilization can stand. But it cannot stand with it either, since terror in the sense of the slaughter of the innocent is properly inimical to it. Terror as a force seeking to destroy peaceable men and women for its own ideological ends has to be countered, if necessary by violence. Yet terror is not, as Pentheus suspects, simply an alien power seeking to invade the city. If it were, it would be far easier to deal with. With the alien you know where you are, namely else-where. It is the otherness at the core of the self which is most troubling, whether one calls this in affirmative mood Dionysian 'inspiration', or the demoniac possession which impels you to rip apart a child.

Dionysus is the god of wine because alcohol both ravages and invigorates. As such, it is a suitable sign of the slippery, ambiguous powers out of which we manufacture our cultures. It is also a sign of oblivion. The wine of Dionysus both consoles and deludes, bringing us those narcotic illusions known as ideology which allow us to forget about labour. Caught in this trance-like delirium, we can put all that dreary material necessity behind us, disavowing the truth that even civilization's most noble achievements have their obscure roots in human wretchedness. This is one reason why Pentheus would do well to strike a bargain with the god. He ought to see that it would be in his own interests for those he governs to be so meekly deluded. In fact, ancient Greece struck just such a canny bargain with Dionysus, as a regulated cult of the god was established alongside the more orthodox worship of Apollo.[9]

The wine of Dionysus brings violence as well as solace in its wake. These drunken fantasies deflate the world at the same time as they inflate the self. Reality becomes magically responsive to one's touch, while individual identity, merged into a frenzied cult, takes on the spurious immortality of the collective. In this infantile condition, enraged as it is by the slightest hint of material resistance, violence becomes ineluctable. In the cult of Dionysus, with its curious mixture of the laid-back and the atrociously bloodthirsty, the regressive roots of power are laid bare. Sensual fantasy swaddles you from the world, thus undoing your inhibitions about pounding it to pieces. We shall see a similar link between sensual decadence and brute force in D. H. Lawrence's *Women in Love*. In this sense, a certain barbarism is actually produced by culture or the pleasure principle.

The claim that culture and barbarism are closely allied is one which distinguishes radicals from both liberals and conservatives. Conservatives greet such a notion with scepticism, whereas liberals tend to regard the violence and exploitation which reared Chartres or Chatsworth as deplorable but finally worth the cost. Radicals, by contrast, do not consider such outcrops of the spirit, whatever their magnificence, as worth the exploitative systems they involved. Splendid as they are, we would have been better off without them. It is not unreasonable to conclude that if humanity meets with some catastrophic finale, its achievements might be judged in retrospect not to have been worth the sufferings they cost. Which is not to say that such cultural treasures, given that we have them, should be disdained, let alone demolished. Only sophisticates go in for such primitivism. It is a very avant-garde sort of atavism. It is rather than we must acknowledge the appalling price which history extorts for what is precious, as Pentheus is finally compelled to do. To acknowledge that, when it comes to civilization, terror in the sense of barbarism goes all the way down is by no means to knuckle under to it. The same goes for political terrorism. It is not a matter of offering Osama bin Laden a seat in Parliament, but of granting justice to those who might otherwise exact a terrible revenge. Justice is the only prophylactic for terror. It is Pentheus's injustice which *The Bacchae* sees as the catalyst of the tragedy, not his chilly self-repression.

The violence which wrests culture out of Nature does not cease once that process is complete. On the contrary, it is needed in the form of military firepower to protect that order from external threat. What was once alien is now known as the army. The monstrous or disruptive must be co-opted by the official and familiar, as the social order comes to harbour a terror at its heart that was once foreboding but is now friendly. A blessing is plucked from a curse, as the violence which risks scuppering civilization is now deployed to preserve it. In Aeschylus's *Oresteia*, the repulsive Furies will become the kindly Eumenides, turning their aggression outward to defend the city-state. In Sophocles's *Oedipus at Colonus*, the polluted Oedipus is transformed into a tutelary deity, protecting the citizens of Athens from assault. Every fairy tale in which the rough beast becomes a handsome prince has its seed in this transfiguration. This means, however, that there is a secret affinity between what founds the state—violence—and what lays siege to it. This is not to claim a moral equivalence between the two: citizens do indeed need safeguarding, by force if necessary, from those who offer to destroy them. Terror has its civilized uses; but it is to be approached with reverence, in fear and trembling. If you are to deploy it effectively, you must acknowledge its duplicitous nature. Otherwise, like Dionysus—the sweetly seductive terror which seeks an allotted place in the social order only to be brusquely sent packing—it is likely to turn on you and tear you apart. Civilization must pay homage to its other, not least because there is a sense in which it lives off it.

It is hard, however, to accommodate such terror without defusing it. In Freudian terms, it must be sublimated—but not so completely that it ceases to remind us of the precariousness and fragility of our existence, its enigmatic origins, its unthinkable ambivalences, the extent to which we are darkly opaque to ourselves. It must inculcate in us an anti-hubristic modesty and moral realism, which is part of what the ancient Greeks meant by piety. But it must not do so to the point where we are crushed by its chastisements, humiliated rather than chastened, plunged into an abysmal lack of self-esteem, and thus cease to function as responsible citizens at all. Terror is essential for the good life, but like the Freudian superego it is always in danger of getting out of hand. Like a tiger, it can never be successfully tamed. From the viewpoint of political order, this is what is both alarming and reassuring about it.

Rather surprisingly, Dionysus upbraids the stiff-necked Pentheus for failing to respect custom and the common wisdom in forbidding his worship. We are not accustomed to hearing orgiastic gods cast their arguments in such Burkeian terms, or to find rapture and reverence so closely allied. What has been long accepted, so the Chorus claims, is what is grounded in human nature, and to question such tradition is the hubris of the errant intellectual. For this drama, as for Burke's thoughts on the French Revolution, there is something deranged or terroristic about the kind of politics which shears through whole sedimented layers of custom and tradition in order to attain its ends. It is the equivalent of demolishing a city in order to save it. What is wrong with the Jacobins in Burke's eyes is what is wrong with Pentheus in Dionysus's view: lack of piety. For all the quaintness of the term, much Western foreign policy today suffers from just the same defect.

The irony of Dionysus's case is that what he sees as having long been socially accepted is a kind of anti-social rupture with the everyday. His point is that the delirious animal joy he represents needs to be revered by being somehow incorporated into the social order. *Jouissance* must be institutionalized. Otherwise we will come to forget that we belong with the beasts, deny our own creatureliness, and court the appalling hubris of a reason torn free from the body. In this sense, celebrating our compact with Nature is the foundation of a thriving culture, not its opposite. Piety is a form of politics.

There is, to be sure, a distinction between the manic *jouissance* or fearful ecstasy of the Bacchic cult, and the sedate *plaisirs* of civilized existence. But if Pentheus had any sense he would find house-room for this libidinal trangression, rather as carnival does. Erotic frenzy is all very well in its place. There is no harm in the odd orgy; on the contrary, there is a power of good to be reaped from it, since to institutionalize the Bacchic rites—to make a custom out of mass copulation—is a tangible sign of acknowledging the ineradicable terror at the heart of social existence. And this moral realism is an essential foundation for human flourishing. In clearing a social space for this terror, the monstrous and the familiar may be reconciled, as they are also, so we shall see later, in the figure of the scapegoat or sacrificial victim. Euripides's play, which never ceases to reflect on the idea of customs and norms, sees that there is something normative about a certain kind of transgression. It is in our natures to be in excess of our natures. There is a surplus to our biological needs and drives which we call culture, and it is this superfluity which makes us the peculiar animals we are. To give the Bacchae house-room would be to acknowledge this fact, and would thus constitute a valuable kind of self-knowledge as well.

To acknowledge this thing of darkness as our own, which is what Pentheus ought to have done when confronted with Dionysus, is not to succumb to some sentimental liberal wisdom. It is not to deny this god's ghastly horror, in some fantasy of inclusivity. Neither is it to draw up a facile equation between state power, which can always be deployed for just ends, and the fury of those who maim the innocent. Once that fury is on the loose, there is no way to protect the city from it except by an answerable force. The death drive is crafty, implacable, vindictive, and bottomlessly malevolent, rejoicing in the sight of gouged eye sockets and the bleeding stumps of limbs. It does not simply endorse such destruction, but actively revels in it. It sucks life from death, growing fat on human carnage. This is why, as we shall see later, those who actively pledge themselves to this force commit deeds which can genuinely be described as evil.

Pentheus, however, had his chance. If he had not treated this bizarre Eastern cult so brutally, he would not have ended up as he does. It is his own violence which results in his mother nursing his severed head on her lap, in the fond illusion that she is cradling a lion cub. Both the Chorus and Cadmus, Pentheus's grandfather, declare that the dismembering of the king is just, which is scarcely the kind of way modern political leaders react to terroristic events on their soil. Nor is it the sort of attitude one would usually take to one's grandson. If they view it as just, however, it is because Pentheus, brushing aside what we might call a 'political' solution to the problem of Dionysus, brought this catastrophe on himself through his own mulishness. It is his arrogant indifference to the ways of those culturally different to himself which has brought him low.

Even so, both Cadmus and the Chorus are worried about the crazed excess of this justice. 'Your revenge is merciless,' Cadmus complains to the god, reminding him that deities should rise above human vindictiveness. And he is surely right. Justice is a matter of symmetry or equitable exchanges, a tit-for-tat logic which abhors surplus or disproportion. The biblical injunction 'An eye for an eye and a tooth for a tooth', commonly cited as the very model of primitive vengeance, is in fact the exact opposite: it urges those offended to seek penalties which are proportionate to the crime. Indeed, it dramatizes the exchange-value logic of justice by pressing it to a literal extreme, as though one were to permit the relatives of the victim of a drunken driver to run the offender over in their turn. It is mercy which is excessive, not justice. As Portia remarks in *The Merchant of Venice*, its quality is 'not strain'd' (unconstrained).

(She does not, however, allow this noble sentiment to interfere with her ruthlessly opportunistic prosecution of Shylock.) Mercy breaks the closed circuit or repetitive tit-for-tat of justice, disrupting the sealed economy of exchange by refusing to return like for like. It is an ethic of incommensurability.

The problem is how this gratuitous gesture is not to undercut an economy of exact exchanges in a way which makes a mockery of justice, an issue which Shakespeare investigates in *Measure for Measure*. Mercy in its superfluity must not look too uncomfortably like vengeance. If authority is to be merciful, there must be a kind of waywardness or irregularity at its heart; but this must not be allowed to undo the law, thus jeopardizing its protection of the weak against the powerful. If the law is to have force, it must feel for the defective flesh and blood on which it passes judgement. Otherwise its judgements, like those of Pentheus, would be flawed by their icy remoteness from such situations. Yet how can the law acknowledge such humanity in itself and still retain its authority? Is what allows the law to grasp the reality of a situation also what disables its judgement of it?

As Shakespeare sees, the vulnerable need the shelter of the law, and would be unwise to rely in this respect on the whims of their superiors. This is why Shylock in *The Merchant of Venice* insists on the letter of his bond, aware in his Jewish way that the letter gives life as well as kills. A properly codified law is essential to safeguard the interests of the weak, whatever the cavalier liberals of the play may consider. Not all superfluity is creative. If mercy and forgiveness are beneficent forms of it, there are destructive ones as well, and *King Lear* devotes much of its time to investigating the hair-thin frontier between the two. There is the 'superfluity' of sheer unmotivated malice, for example, as in the case of *Othello*'s Iago. In any case, those who forgive easily may do so because, like Lucio in *Measure for Measure*, they are airily indifferent to moral value in the first place. And people who buy their forgiveness on the cheap are for the same reason incapable of being truly forgiven. Barnadine, the play's death-row psychopath, is such a character, a man so morally torpid that he is reluctant to be woken up in order to be executed. The state needs this monster of moral inertia to repent—which is to say, to internalize the law and make some sense of his own death—if it is to avoid being made a fool of.

Yet justice can be excessive as well, as *The Bacchae* tragically demonstrates. So for that matter does Heinrich von Kleist's extraordinary story *Michael Kohlhaas*, whose eponymous hero sets fire to Wittenberg three times, attacks Leipzig, refuses peace overtures from Martin Luther, and defeats or outflanks a whole series of military expeditions launched against him, and all because a couple of his horses have been stolen. The case, having embroiled entire state apparatuses and caused countless deaths, ends up before the Holy Roman Emperor. It is perhaps no coincidence that Kleist, poet of extremity, is also the author of a remarkably fine drama of Amazonian women, *Penthesilia*, which like *The Bacchae* is an extraordinary blending of violence and eroticism, tenderness and aggression. Penthesilia, who believes in kissing men with steel and hugging them to death, speaks in one modern-day translation of a kiss and a bite being pretty much 'cheek by jowl', and regrets tearing with her teeth at Achilles as 'a slip of the tongue'.[10]

Justice, then, can be quite as lunatic as revenge. There is something properly absolute about it, which can easily become intransigent. There is a smack of such surreal stiff-neckedness about both Sophocles's Antigone and Shakespeare's Shylock. The ways of heaven are supposed to rebuke this obduracy: you are not permitted to lay waste a town because its insurgents have murdered some of your own soldiers, or bomb a packed marketplace because a child has been slaughtered. Yet the gods themselves are creatures of excess—partly because their logic, if they have any, is bound to exceed our understanding, but also because, in the case of Judaeo-Christianity at least, Yahweh is boundless in his love and mercy, and all boundlessness is potentially a form of terror. This is why, on one rather crude theological view, an infinite (and so humanly intolerable) God needs diplomatically to conceal himself in the finite flesh and blood of his son, rather as an intellectual might try to avoid intimidating his cleaning lady by adopting her accent.

Dionysus is the god of surplus—of activities like sex, theatre, drinking, and dancing, which have no need to justify themselves before some sour-faced tribunal of social utility. In this sense, then, he is the patron saint of culture—of all that is not defined by its practical social function. Yet the sheer malignancy of the death drive has no utilitarian point either, which is one reason why Dionysus represents both. If excess signifies a joy beyond the reach of buttoned-down bureaucrats like Pentheus, it also means Pentheus's mother Agave wrenching her son's arm from its socket while foaming wildly at the mouth.

Human bodies are comically interchangeable in an orgy, but tragically so in a terrorist bombing or concentration camp. As far as both the predatory and the promiscuous go, any old body will do. You are not granted even the meagre dignity of being decapitated by a suicide bomber because you are you. In massacres as in mass orgies, everyone is just a stand-in for everyone else. Both kinds of event exemplify the abstract logic of modernity. Dionysus is all about identity, but only in the sense of merging individuals indifferently into one. This god signifies the death of difference. It is true that in sabotaging the falsely autonomous selfhood of a Pentheus ('You do not know what you are saying, what you do, nor who you are', Dionysus tells him), the Bacchic cult challenges a noxious form of political authority. Pentheus will know who he is not when his identity grows luminously clear to him, but when he recognizes that it involves a blindness which cannot be wholly dissipated. The same is true of the repentant Oedipus, whose knowledge will end up putting out his eyes. The cult also questions too-assured sexual identities. Dionysus himself is glamorously epicene, and Pentheus moves under his spell from tyrant to transvestite. What might nowadays be voguishly called getting in touch with the woman within himself turns out to mean getting in touch with the mass murderer.

Even so, Euripides is no postmodernist. *The Bacchae* sees how frighteningly close a creative troubling of identity is to a brutal liquidation of it. Dionysus is all about decentring the subject, but in a monolithic, pathological sort of way. Drunks may be liberated from constraints, but this is not what we call freedom, a practice for which some sort of ego is required. The Bacchic revellers are positive slaves to emancipation, as driven in their pleasures as any compulsive neurotic. The Dionysian death drive, like the totalitarian state, offers us the seductive prospect of shedding our separate egos, and thus of healing the hurt which individuation entails. Like the black hole of the Real, it obliterates differences.

Yet the injuries we endure in being severed from Nature are also the precondition of historical fulfilment, as opposed to the more impoverished business of animal pleasure. It is in this sense that this severance is a fortunate Fall or *felix culpa*. Self-hood is born of a well-nigh unbearable sacrifice—one which we will no more outgrow than infancy, but which persists as an obscure bruise at the very pith of identity. Yet only through this sacrifice is it possible to conceive of a happiness which might be shorn of violence. Meanwhile, as Euripides's Chorus insists, the cult of Dionysus must be granted formal recognition. Even if the bliss of the beasts is not for us, the Bacchae are there to remind us that our happiness, too, is of a creaturely kind. It is in this sense that Dionysus is a utopian figure as well as a regressive one. But it has to be a form of happiness appropriate to our peculiar kind of creatureliness, which is where the god proves disastrously deficient. It is not that the fulfilments peculiar to us are 'spiritual' rather than animal; it is rather that they belong to that mode of animality known as the ethical, which is to say that they involve questions of the fulfilment or non-fulfilment of others. It is because we can reflect on how far our own happiness might baulk that of others, or vice versa, that we can in principle achieve more intricate, all-round enjoyments than the brutally orgasmic Dionysus has to offer. In the end, the moral responsibility to which he is a stranger involves augmenting our pleasures, not diminishing them.

Even so, because this is indeed only in the end, the Dionysians can lord it over the rest of us as far as sheer delight goes. They could point out, too, that though our pleasures may be more subtle and delicate than their own, they will always be haunted by a primordial unhappiness born of being ripped from our mindless communion with the world. To this extent, they have a persuasive case. Would even the finest of historical fulfilments compensate for the loss of Eden? It may be that an ecstatic self-dissolution into Nature is a bogus sort of joy, since (as Keats recognizes in the *Ode to a Nightingale*) there would be nobody around to experience it. Yet what if we exchange this for an existence which merely succeeds in enhancing our cruelty along with our flourishing? Could Dionysus be right in his view that we would be better off if the Fall, however *felix*, had never happened?

'Most terrible, although most gentle, to mankind', is how Dionysus describes himself. 'At once your cruellest enemy, and your dearest friend', are Agave's words of mourning to the corpse of the son she has loved and destroyed. It is the familiar ambiguity of the sacred—of those Janus-faced powers which are both intimate and alien, affectionate and inhuman. The cult of Dionysus is in one sense a denial of otherness, to which it opposes an implacable self-identity; yet since this remorseless force installs itself as a stranger at the very quick of the self, in what the ancients knew as prophetic inspiration, otherness is not so much denied as internalized. At the core of the self lies a power which makes it what it is, yet which is unutterably foreign to it. Historically speaking, this power has been endowed with many names: the gods, God, the sublime, freedom, Spirit, History, Will, the life-force, language, power, the unconscious, the Other, the Real. What most of these share in common is a degree of terror. There is an 'angelic' current of Western thought for which the self and the anonymous powers which constitute it are in principle in harmony, and a tragic or 'demonic' strain of theory for which, since we come into our own through the Other, identity itself is a matter of self-estrangement.

Because the death drive actually commands us to enjoy our own dismemberment, it is the place where the opposition between law and desire, superego and id, is most dramatically dismantled. This is why Dionysus, in a positive riot of per-versity, is both autocrat and anarchist, god and rebel, judge and outlaw. In a superb irony, this lawless liberationist punishes Pentheus the king for having kicked over the traces. Law and desire are locked in lethal complicity—in Pentheus's case, because by denying his desire he monstrously increases it; in Dionysus's case, because desire stands revealed as a cruelly compulsive law all of its own, as blind and coercive as the most imperious edict. Absolute power is mad with desire, seized by an insatiable lust to dominate and destroy. Its exponents are criminals because their actions fall outside the law, but also because since they are the law's masters, they cannot be subject to it. In this sense, sovereign and rebel are at one.

Many Christian theologians would now regard it as a mistake to speak of God in moral terms. God is not well-behaved. He is not a moral being, since morality is only for those who need to work out the complex historical implications of love, a tiresome affair from which the Almighty is presumably dispensed. Like a minor member of royalty, God has no duties whatsoever. In a similar way, the gods of antiquity are not moral either—not because they are immoral, though they are sometimes spectacu-larly so, but because there is a sense in which the discourse of morality has no more bearing on them than it has on a sand-storm. There is no more question of celebrating or condemning Dionysus than there is of celebrating or condemning the planet Neptune. It is rather a question of acknowledging the way things are with humanity—of registering the immortal presence of Eros and Thanatos, and the dreadful consequences which may follow for those who turn their eyes self-righteously from them.

When Cadmus upbraids Dionysus for his extremism, the god simply ripostes that his father Zeus ordained it all from the beginning. This is less a moral evasion than an appeal to the limits of such moral categories. A certain extremism is built into the way things are with us; and though this is no good reason to rip your child's arm from its shoulder, there is a limit to the extent to which moral norms can moderate it. Those who fail to recognize this extremity for what it is—those who cannot stomach the truth that this monstrous urge to self-destruction is, like most forms of monstrosity, part of the latent stuff of everyday life—are likely to be lacking in reverence, and so likely in the end to enhance the violence. You may forget about Eros and Thanatos, but you can be sure that they will not forget about you. This, one might claim, is more realism than fatalism—but even if it is fatalism, it is of the kind which proves useful for discrediting those for whom the moral life is all about options. It touches on a certain ineluctability in things, one which is scandalous to those contemporary thinkers who are in love with the contingent, the random, the perpetually protean (and whose only interest in Pentheus would no doubt be that he appears at one point in drag). Such theorists assume that ineluctability is bound to be a bad thing, which is by no means the case. There are many forms of inevitability which are benign.

Pentheus may help to trigger the very madness he fears, but that does not make the forces he unleashes any less horrifying. He may demonize Dionysus, but that does not mean that the god is not a devil already. The line between gods and demons is notoriously hard to draw, and rarely more so than in this case. The Theban ruler makes things a lot worse by his parochialism and cackhandedness, but there is no guarantee that a political compromise could have been pulled off. Even so, *The Bacchae* insists on the deep affinity between terrorism and injustice. Pentheus is destroyed because he refuses to welcome the stranger, closing his gates to an alien power which is both subversive and redemptive. Authoritarians like him can see dissidence only as anarchy, and by stamping on it as hard as they do they become self-fulfilling prophets.

The fundamentalist, whether Texan or Taliban, is the flipside of the nihilist: both parties believe that nothing has meaning or value unless it is founded on cast-iron first principles. It is just that the fundamentalist believes in such principles, whereas the nihilist does not. The secret collusion between Pentheus and Dionysus, sworn enemies and terrible twins, is an image of this alliance. For fundamentalists, the choice is between anarchy and absolute truth. They do not see that this is a self-confirming proposition, since for absolutism anything short of itself is bound to look anarchic. Anarchy and absolutism are the recto and verso of each other. Both suspect that chaos is our natural condition. It is just that absolutists fear it, whereas anarchists revel in it. But the latter also leads to the former, since an inherently disorderly world invites the smack of firm government. Champions of the gloriously unruly do not recognize that only a world inherently susceptible to order can be other than arbitrarily violent.

Since Dionysus is the god of tragedy, *The Bacchae* is a play not only about him but in honour of him. Like the Bacchic rite, tragic art is a perverse blend of terror and delight. Because the tragic catastrophe is cast in sublimated or symbolic form, the spectators of the drama feel unthreatened enough to reap pleasure from it. In drawing life from the downfall of others, we can flirt with death secure in the knowledge that we cannot actually be harmed. We can vicariously gratify our self-destructive drives, at the same time as we can indulge in a certain sadistic pleasure at the prospect of others' pain.[11] Tragedy is in this sense a gentrified, socially acceptable version of obscene enjoyment, as well as an art-form of great moral depth and splendour. Like the Dionysus to whom it is dedicated, it is an uncanny mixture of the intimate and the alien—or as Aristotle would say, of pity and fear.

If there is identity, there is also estrangement, as with those Dionysian devotees who harbour a monster at the core of the self. We feel for the tragic protagonist, whose calamities recall us to a sense of our own frailty and finitude. Yet if we affirm our solidarity with this mutilated figure, which is what Aristotle calls pity, we are also appalled by the terror which tears him apart, which is what Aristotle calls fear. Through his sufferings, we act out a symbolic openness to our own mortality; yet because it is he, not us, who dies, this humility is laced with a triumphant sense of our own immortality. Tragedy is among other things a fantasy of eternal life—not only because it is we spectators who are the survivors, but because the tragic hero himself, in accepting his death, testifies in his courage to a spirit which cannot be broken by it. His destruction is thus both victory and failure, submission and transcendence. We shall be looking at a modern-day version of this paradox a little later, in the figure of the suicide bomber.

If Dionysus is one example of holy terror in pagan antiquity, the prime example of it in the Middle Ages is God. For Judaeo-Christian thought, God is a flaming fire who is terrible to look on. His pitiless love knows no bounds and is alarmingly unconditional. What repudiates all compromise here is not power but mercy. This remorseless force casts down the mighty and raises up the lowly, fills the hungry with good things and sends the rich empty away, without pausing for political negotiations. For those who cannot take it, divine love looms up as a raging fire of destruction, generally known as the fire of hell. St Augustine speaks in his *Confessions* of God as 'one who fills me with terror and burning love: with terror in so much as I am utterly other than it, with love in that I am akin to it'.[12] God is both pure otherness, yet (in Thomas Aquinas's view) closer to us than we are to ourselves. In a strange sort of Trinitarian incest, he is our brother as well as our father. His invisibility is not that of a remote celestial object, but that of a medium like light, too close and pervasive to be objectified. He is invisible because he is the ground and source of our seeing, rather than an object within our visual field.

Human law has both a kindly and an intimidatory face. This is not a contradiction it can escape, since it must resort to force to protect the powerless who take shelter beneath it. Even so, it is a contradiction which threatens to strip the law of the credibility and free assent it needs in order to be effective, since our minds are not easily adapted to a power which is at once daunting and benign. If the law has an angelic presence, it also has a Satanic one. This would then seem true of God as well, whom we are expected both to love and fear. Yet the parallel is deceptive, for what is most fearful about God is his love. God is a shattering, traumatic, sweetly intolerable force who breaks and remakes human subjects by offering them something of his own frighteningly unconditional friendship. Fearing God does not mean being scared witless by his implacable wrath but respecting his law, which is the law of justice and compassion. Since, however, we are not up to living unconditionally like him—since our own affections are bound to be conditional—failure is built into this project, which is why divine love is also forgiveness. Failure is not a problem, since in this particular game there was never any chance of success in the first place.

If God's love is itself a traumatizing, disruptive demand, then it has the force of a law, and the opposition between law and love is accordingly dismantled. To be 'converted' is to come to recognize that the horrific Real at the core of the self, the unfathomable strangeness which makes us what we are, is not after all unfriendly. This Real can be seen among other things as a destructive antagonism-cum-collusion between law and desire; and what breaks this vicious circle, in which the law obtusely provokes a desire which it then goes on to punish, is the recognition that the law or Name-of-the Father is itself desirous—but desirous in the sense that it wants our well-being, and is thus a kind of love. In the Real of Dionysus, law and desire become lethally entangled, as we are brutally commanded to lay violent hands on ourselves. With God, however, law and love are not at loggerheads. Love turns out to have the disruptive, traumatic, uncompromising quality of law, while law—since it is the law of justice—is revealed as carnal, affirming a solidarity with suffering flesh and blood. This is part of what it means to call Jesus the Son of God. He is the 'son' of God because he is the authentic rather than ideological image of the Father, revealing him as comrade, lover, and counsel for the defence rather than as patriarch, judge, and accuser. It is Jesus's broken body which is the signifier of the law. Those who are faithful to the law of the Father and speak up for justice will be done away with by the state.

The Hebrew word for 'accuser' is 'Satan'. Satan is the pathologized image of God cultivated by those for whom love is an intolerable weakness, and who need to think instead in terms of power and sovereignty. The devil is the enemy of God in the sense that he is an ideological misreading of him. He is the totem of those who cannot accept that the Real which the tortured body of Jesus shows up the divine law to be is not the obscenity of sadistic power, but an obscenity of a different kind—the frightful image of God himself as vulnerable animal and bloody scapegoat, the flayed and butchered *pharmakos* of Calvary. In being 'made sin', in St Paul's phrase, this humiliated creature enters into suffering solidarity with all the mutilated victims of what St John dismissively calls the powers of this world, powers whose death knell has now struck.

This *pharmakos* makes its descent into the hell of the Real in order to show up its kernel of inhumanity not as that of an oppressive law, but as the inhumanity of destitution—the condition in which by being less than ourselves, divested of our natures, we manifest what is most constitutive of them. It is not a matter of the human versus the inhuman, but of one kind of inhumanity against another. To claim that, say, Auschwitz is beyond tragedy is to say that unless we react to its horror with our familiar responses of pity, outrage, compassion, and the like, we risk being collusive with its inhumanity—yet that at a different level these common-or-garden responses are shown up by the event as really quite irrelevant, so that only a humanity which had passed beyond humanity, and in doing so had become more rather than less human, would be on answerable terms with it. We shall be looking again to this notion of a humanity beyond the human when we come to examine D. H. Lawrence's *Women in Love*.

Law and love, then, are not alternatives. Mercy and forgiveness are binding and obligatory, not optional extras. Edmund Burke, who as we shall see later saw law and affection as near neighbours in the sublime, declared that charity is 'a direct and obligatory duty'.[13] It is only anti-Semitic Christians who oppose law to love, defining the Judaic law as callously legalistic so that they can contrast its strictures unfavourably with their own tender hearts. There is indeed something inhuman about the law, but so is there about love. The command to love is a traumatic one because it is a universal imperative, and thus is bound to be implacably indifferent to the individual—not to his or her specific person, to be sure, but indifferent to which specific person is in question. We are commanded to love indiscriminately, which is why the paradigmatic case of such conduct is the love of strangers. Anybody can love a friend.

Rather as the law can grant no favours to the socially privileged ('privileged' meaning 'private law'), so love is no respecter of persons. It is only because we have narrowed its meaning to the erotic variety that we fail to notice this. Nor is love any respecter of cultures, however dismayed postmodernism may be to hear it. What is injurious about it, among other things, is its ruthless abstraction. It is precisely not the opposite of abstract universalism, whatever neo-Romantics may imagine. Yet neither is it the opposite of particularity. It is indeed devoted to the needs of uniquely particular individuals. It is just that this devotion is entirely promiscuous. One can contrast this with erotic love. As we have seen in the case of Dionysus, Eros is a matter of drives which are ruthlessly indifferent to individual persons. There is something inhuman about sexuality, as one would expect from a power which binds us so closely to Nature. Desire is nothing personal. But Eros is also a matter of romantic love, in which an irreducibly particular person is elevated to sublime status. For *agape*, or political love as we might translate the term, the personal and impersonal are interwoven in a different way, in the 'inhuman', unreasonable command to attend to the personal needs of any individual whatsoever.

In words which prefigure the New Testament, Dionysus presents himself as a god whose yoke is easy. Rest, not labour, is his gift to a humanity wearied by toil. He is not the old, irascible sort of deity, as full of whimsical demands and eccentric requirements as a rock star. Yet if Yahweh's yoke is easy, it is not quite because he encourages his acolytes to lounge around all day in various interesting postures of *jouissance*. It is true that Jesus's vagabond, footloose condition is a scandal to the more suburban-minded citizens of first-century Palestine. A scourge of property and productivity, he urges his followers to live like the lilies of the field and take no thought for tomorrow. Yet Jesus's homelessness, to which he specifically draws attention, is more an assault on family values than a Bacchic lifestyle. He has harsh words for an intending recruit who asks to say goodbye to his parents between joining up, and tells his disciples brutally that the choice is between their mothers, fathers, brothers, and sisters, whom they must 'hate', and himself. As a child, he refuses to apologize to his distraught parents for wandering off, insisting that his public mission takes priority over domestic loyalties. When his mother and brothers show up in the crowd and request to see him in private, he tells them abruptly to wait. When a woman in the crowd speaks up loudly in praise of the womb which bore him, he ripostes with an acidic put-down. He has come, he declares, as a sword to divide households and set family members at each other's throats. The Real which he signifies disrupts the symbolic order, driving a coach and horses through the conventional structures of kinship. The New Testament is notably hostile to family values.

As one who consorts amicably with whores, Jesus has strikingly little to say about sex, and his minders are horrified to catch him speaking alone to a sexually promiscuous Samaritan woman. A holy man of the time with a reputation to keep up would not be caught speaking without a chaperone with a woman, even a respectable one, and least of all with a Samaritan, Samaritans being a socially disreputable bunch despised by most Jews of the time. It is this abrasive critique of family values which in the hands of their conservative champions has now become the most lethal text on the planet.

Dionysus offers men and women precious time off from their burdensome existence under the political law. We have seen already that such carnivalesque interludes are in the interests of the governing powers rather than an affront to them. As Olivia observes in *Twelfth Night*, there is no slander in an allowed Fool, no harm in jesters so long as they are licensed. When transgression is ordained, deviancy becomes the norm and the demonic finds itself baffled and redundant. This is why the devil finds himself with empty hands in the postmodern world. If Jesus's law is light, however, it is not only because he, too, comes to relieve the labouring poor of their afflictions, but because God commands nothing more of his people than that they should allow him to love them. Because he is the Other who neither lacks nor desires, unlike the Lacanian variety, he needs nothing from others, and his law is consequently free of neurotic compulsion and paranoid possessiveness. Ironically, it is God's transcendence—the fact that he is complete in himself, has no need of the world, and created it out of love rather than need—that allows him to go so easy on his creatures.

God himself has the necessity of a law, in that his being is not contingent. But this law, once again, is the law of love—for since nothing apart from God needs to exist, whatever does exist does so gratuitously, as a result of his unmotivated generosity. To say that things were created out of nothing means that they did not have to come about. They did not follow inexorably from some precedent, as elements of a causal or logical chain. Creation, in Alain Badiou's terms, is an 'event', not a dreary necessity.[14] The cosmos could quite easily never have happened. Instead, God could have devoted his considerable talents to, say, figuring out how to create square circles. To claim that things are 'created' is to claim that they are pure gift or contingency. There is no necessity for the House of Lords or the Grand Canyon. The gratuitousness of things, *pace* the existentialists, is an argument in favour of God, not against him.

Since religious fundamentalism is among other things an inability to accept contingency, the universe itself is a persuasive argument against such a creed. What fundamentalism finds hard to stomach is that nothing whatsoever needs to exist, least of all ourselves. For St Augustine, the fact that human beings are 'created' means that their being is shot through with non-being. Like some modernist works of art, we are riddled from end to end with the scandal of our own non-necessity. Since this is a potentially debilitating condition, ideology exists among other things to convince us that we are needed. It posits an internal bond between ourselves and the world. Otherwise, dispirited by a sense of our own contingency, we might fail to rise from our beds, which would be bad news for the Chancellor of the Exchequer.

It is this gratuitousness of God that the Pharisees are unable to swallow.[15] Confronted with the enigmatic Other, the Lacanian subject raises one anxious query after another: 'What do you want of me? How can I know what you desire? How can

I become what you desire me to be? Is it me you want, or something in me?' These are also the impeccably well-behaved Pharisee's enquiries of God: 'Have you any more dietary regulations for me to observe? When will you be satisfied with me? Would 1 per cent of my income donated to charity be enough to guarantee salvation?' If God remains inscrutably silent in the face of these clamorous demands, it is because the morally reputable citizen is asking the wrong questions, as so many who stood before the cryptic features of the Sphinx returned the wrong answers. He cannot acknowledge the scandal that the demand of the Other here is purely empty, the phatic Hebrew phrase 'Here I am!' rather than a meticulous set of requirements. Like the psychotic, he cannot accept that the Other is necessarily invisible, not just accidentally so; that it is not to be imaged or totalized; and that a certain iconoclasm is thus the only appropriate response to its (non)presence. Instead, the Pharisee demands a determinate image of the Other in order to guarantee his own being. In St Augustine's view, those who like the Pharisees are virtuous simply because the law requires it of them are not really free, just as I am not a responsible citizen if I refrain from breaking your jaw simply because I have a terror of the sound of police sirens.

For St Paul, it is not that love liquidates the law, but that it replaces an ideological misreading of it with an authentic one. No doubt this is what Jesus has in mind when he remarks that he has come not to abolish the law but to fulfil it. He has come to disclose the true nature of the law—to reveal it as death-dealing not in the sense of driving us gleefully to our graves, but in the sense that holding out for the justice which it demands is likely to lead to political execution. Paul speaks in his letter to the Galatians of the 'curse of the law', which coming from a former Pharisee is quite a turn-about; but he is, after all, a devout first-century Jew rather than a postmodern Parisian philosopher. He is not the kind of politically irresponsible theorist who regards all law as darkly authoritarian, while no doubt feeling mightily relieved that the police have just managed to track down his child's kidnappers.

Paul's attitude to the Mosaic law is rather more subtle than the banal belief that all authority is oppressive and elitist. For him, the Mosaic law is not cursed *tout court*. How could it be if it is the law of God? It is, rather, both cursed and holy, and thus yet another example of the ambivalence of the sacred. This is because it is indeed the law of love, but, so to speak, a version of it for beginners. It is propaedeutic rather than an end in itself. It spells out what we ought to do—but the fact that it needs to do so is already an ominous sign of our frailty. A child faced with a list of prohibitions tends understandably to treat them as ends in themselves. It is hard for it to grasp that 'Do not bully!', 'Do not play football with Max's lunchbox!' and the like are, so to speak, the scaffolding of a virtuous way of life rather than the thing itself. The child might well find itself at a loss to know how to go about obeying more positive injunctions such as 'Treat others considerately!'

It is not, then, that the moral law is pernicious, but that if we could really live according to its injunctions we would no longer have need of them. The technical term for this is grace. One speaks or dances gracefully when one no longer needs to keep thinking about the rules. One would not trust a driver who kept the Highway Code open on his lap. As Aristotle is aware, virtue is something we have to get good at, like tolerating noisy neighbours or playing the tin whistle. Once we have climbed this ladder of the law, however, we can throw it away; only then will we see the world aright. Like radical politics, the law must contain a self-destruct device: once it has brought about its goal, it ceases to be relevant and can wither away.

The law is our friend because its whole effort is to bring us to this exciting yet alarming point. It is like a parent who understands that the most precious gift she can give her child is that of independence. No longer to be needed will be the sign of her success. Or it is like an actor who has mastered his part and so can dispense with the script. In this way, the law is fulfilled and abolished at the same time. Until that time, however, the law makes itself felt as a kind of stymieing self-consciousness, a dull internal bruising which disrupts our spontaneity, jolts us with a guilty start out of our mindless pleasures, and intrudes in its clumsily mechanistic fashion on our freedom. It is a kind of skewing which puts us out of synchrony with ourselves, and in this sense is as much a curse as a crippling bout of shyness.

It was Nietzsche, of all improbable characters, who saw the moral law most clearly in this light. 'Profoundest gratitude for that which morality has achieved hitherto,' he remarks in *The Will to Power*, 'but now it is only a burden which may become a fatality!'[16] In Nietzsche's unabashedly teleological vision, the moral law was necessary in its day for disciplining and refining human beings, modulating their bullish animal drives into the delicate intricacies of civilized life; but to be fulfilled it must now be overthrown, as the *Übermensch* comes to bestow freely upon himself a law to which men and women previously submitted as to a blindly coercive power.

But this is not to dismiss the era of the moral law as unproductive. Nietzsche is not a naive libertarian, unlike many of his modern-day disciples. The cringing, self-lacerating subject of moral ideology, one which reaps perverse stimulation from its own self-contempt, wins his admiration as well as his censure. This cravenly self-torturing creature Moral Man, with its sickly sado-masochism, hypocritically disavowed instincts, and festering culture of guilt, is also in his eyes the foundation of all civilized achievement and an indispensable bridge to the future domain of freedom. Humanity needs this moral adolescence if it is to pass beyond itself. There is something beautiful as well as despicable about the bad conscience.

The law is cursed because it rubs our noses in our failings simply by existing. Our consciousness of the law is our consciousness of our violation of it. It is because the law defines what counts as transgression in the first place that it necessarily presents itself to us as Satanic—as the baleful power which brings violence and corruption into the world. Without the law, there would be no sin. An Irish scholar wrote proudly in 1684 that the Iar Connacht region of Galway was so law-abiding that none of its inhabitants had been brought to court or executed for thirty years. He forgot to add that the rule of law in the district was not sufficiently well-defined for its subjects to be capable of infringing it with any certainty. By showing us how shoddy we are, the moral law diminishes our self-love to the point where we slide deeper into self-destructive guilt, and so become even less capable of living up to its intractable demands. It splits us between a knowledge of what we ought to do and our gloomy awareness of how little we are up to doing it.

This is not the fault of the law. It is simply that it cannot fulfil its role without generating these unintended consequences. Because love does not come easily or naturally, the law is needed to train us up in its habits and protocols. But this is quite likely to seem a fairly heartless matter. It would be hard, for example, for an outsider confronted with a company's non-smoking policy documents to conclude that these drearily bureaucratic sub-clauses and pedantic morsels of small print are ultimately all in the name of human flourishing and fulfilment. Or—to adopt a more pertinent Lacanian example—it is hard for the small infant to recognize in the parent's practical attention to its needs an expression of his or her love. Is this love or law, kindness or duty? we can imagine the infant wondering anxiously to itself, as being washed or kept warm both reveals and conceals the parent's affection.

The law's education in the ways of love is bound to backfire, which is why the law is such a curse. This is partly because to encode the law in writing opens up the possibility of turning it into a fetish, as Shylock makes a fetish of his bond. He does so because as an oppressed Jew he needs this scrupulously worded contract for his protection, and would be foolish to rely on the hermeneutical vagaries of the Venetian Christian

Establishment. It may be the spirit of the law which counts, but there is no spirit without a letter, no signified without a material signifier. The spirit of the law is an effect of the signifier, not a substitute for it. It is a matter of the creative interpretation of letters, not the spontaneous divining of something lurking bodilessly behind them. Otherwise the spirit of the law could include pretty well any arbitrary implication which sprang to mind, which would be to make a mockery of legality. The 'spirit' of the law must be the spirit of *this* letter. It is not a question of ditching the letter for the spirit, but of grasping the letter of the law *as* spirit and meaning, rather than, say, as some numinous icon in its own right—some totem or mantra which has merely to be magically chanted or brandished to have its effect. In *The Merchant of Venice*, Portia, confronted with the political embarrassment of Shylock's bond, does precisely this: by reading its wording too literally (the text mentions nothing about taking blood, as opposed to flesh, from Antonio), she comes up with a farcical travesty of it. In violating the spirit of Shylock's bond, she treats its letter as dead rather than living, and is consequently unfaithful to it.

The law is thus necessarily at odds with itself—but only, as it were, while we are still in our moral infancy, which means, given our deficiencies, all of the time. Paul views the transition from law to love as a passage from childhood to maturity. But this is a shift in ways of acting and understanding, rather than a move from one dispensation to another. Only Christian anti-Semitism, for which the cold-hearted legal pedantry of the Old Testament yields ground to the warm-hearted spiritual inwardness of the New, claims that. The moment of conversion comes when love dispels the false consciousness which blinded us to the realization that love was what the law was about all along. The scandal of Jesus is not that he breaks the Mosaic law (which by and large he does not), but that he seems to lay claim to authorship of it. If he obeys it himself, then, it is not because he has to, but because he believes it to be life-giving once its real meaning is manifest. That manifestation is his own life and death.

This crisis of conversion finds a parallel in *anagnorisis*, or the moment of tragic recognition. In some rather rarefied forms of tragic theory, the hero rebels against what he sees as an unjust power only to be worsted by it. There can be no defeating destiny. Yet in actively appropriating his defeat, the protagonist reveals a resolution which is a match for the forces which bring him low. For the tragic protagonist to accept his own death must demand at least as unswerving a will as the forces which seek to destroy him. His failure throws his weakness and mortality into stark exposure; but in making his limits plain, it hints, if only negatively, at the infinity which lies beyond them. It is an infinity which can be illuminated only by negation—by the devouring flames in which the hero is consumed. By freely submitting to ineluctable failure, he reveals a boundlessness in himself which is at one with the august powers against which he struggles. Only a power from beyond the hero's creaturely existence could enable him to relinquish that existence. The act of drawing a limit to one's own capabilities must somehow spring from beyond them. On the battleground of his body, then, two kinds of infinity fight it out, and are shown to be secretly one.

In this sense, the tragic act is a kind of performative contradiction, since it transcends in its freedom the very constraints to which it submits. By presiding ceremonially over his own death, becoming both priest and victim, the protagonist succeeds in overcoming his own mortality. The act of free assent by which he makes his destiny his choice allows him to rise above that destiny, demonstrating that it is not, after all, the last word. It reveals the truth that liberty is deeper than necessity—and that if this is so, then the inexorable law to which the hero submits, if it is indeed the highest sovereignty, must itself be freedom in the guise of fate. In dying, then, the hero shows the law in whose name he perishes to be secretly on his side. What looks like barbarous coercion turns out to be a force for justice.

Yet it takes a certain steadfastness in the face of death to make this truth manifest. This tragic paradigm is modelled among other things on the crucifixion of Christ—an event in which Christ's fidelity to the law of the Father is itself an example of infinite love, and thus a revelation of the Father himself. In this way, the death of Jesus overthrows the Satanic image of God as Nobodaddy, superego, or bloodthirsty despot. On this Satanic reading, for which Calvary is the problem rather than the solution, the crucifixion stages the lethal deadlock or entanglement of law and desire, as the sadistic moral law incites desire into motion only because it has already cynically pre-calculated its defeat. The Father summons Jesus to launch his mission of love knowing that it will result in his death, and thus, through his son's perfect obedience, in his own glorification. For his part, Jesus masochistically wills his own destruction, conscious that in the obscene enjoyment of his own death the sublime law of his Father will shine victoriously forth.

The non-Satanic reading of the event, by contrast, sees it as deconstructing the deadly conflict between law and love, which is why it represents a victory over sin. What brings Jesus to his death is not the law of the Father, which is the law of justice and mercy, but the state. It is because Jesus is at one with the law of the Father—is, as they say, the 'son' of the Father—that he is first tortured and then murdered. It is justice which is transgressive. St Paul associates the tyranny of the law with death; but this particular death shows the law up as friendly. In this narrative, it is the Father who rebels against injustice, angrily defying the powers of this world by raising up his murdered child.

Christians such as John Milton, who find this dethroning of the deity hard to stomach, can always opt instead for a view of the crucifixion as the legalistic placating of a vengeful patriarch. For this rather warped theology, God is a terrorist who demands the blood of his own son as the price for having been immortally offended. Even two-legged terrorists can be less insanely excessive than that. There is, even so, a connection between terror and injustice in divine matters as well as in political ones. For the Pharisees of every age, God is indeed a terrorist—though one who might just be bought off by sustained bouts of exceptionally upright conduct, not to speak of the sedulous observance of various esoteric rites. Such men and women fear God in the way one might fear rabies or tarantulas; they do not fear him in the sense of nurturing a reverence for his remorseless thirst for justice. In this sense, those who deny the God of justice are bound to see him as an unholy terror, rather as those who deny justice in political affairs are likely these days to provoke carnage and chaos.

2

States of Sublimity

FOR Thomas Aquinas, God is a kind of nothingness about whom nothing really intelligible can be said, even if Aquinas himself managed to say it at extraordinary length. There is a sense in which he would have endorsed Lenin's scathing comment that theology is 'a subject without an object'. God for Judaeo-Christian theology is not an object, principle, entity, or existent being. He is rather what makes these things possible in the first place. He defeats all representation and strikes language dumb—which is to say, in aesthetic terms, that he is sublime. The only conceivable image of him is human love, a tarnished metaphor at best. Yahweh is a kind of abyss—yet he is, as we have seen, a peculiarly bruising, traumatizing sort of vacancy.

This paradox of a violent void or abrasive form of nothingness returns in late modernity under the name of the Real. This, to be sure, is the 'bad' late-modern or postmodern sublime; the 'good' one is to be found in the postmodern celebration of whatever defeats representation. Psychoanalysis, in other words, is the latest inheritor of the lineage we are tracing. We have moved from the godly to the genital. Psychoanalytic theory is the modern-day heir of theology not only in the institutional sense—it has popes, priests, sects, schisms, laypersons (or patients), confessionals, excommunications, esoteric knowledge, rituals of redemption, and the like—but in the radical depth of the questions it poses. What is the truth of the human subject? Can its existence be justified, or is it doomed to perpetual guilt? Why are we guilty without having done wrong? What do men and women really desire? What is the relationship between law and love? Can I ever be accepted by the Other for what I am? Just as James Joyce once remarked that he was a scholastic in everything but the premises, so psychoanalytic thought acknowledges in the human an unstaunchable infinity of desire, thus rebuffing all ideologies of liberal hope or rationalist consolation, while insisting in the teeth of theology that it is this desire, not its fulfilment in divine love, which is the true eternity. Or, in short, that there is no Other of the Other.

In this insistence, psychoanalysis can be seen as an ultimately tragic creed, whereas Christianity has a rather more ambiguous relation to tragedy. It holds that those who do not accept that the truth of history is a tortured political criminal are idle fantasists, whether they pass under the name of conservative, idealist, or liberal rationalist; but that to accept that this is the last word is also to begin to see beyond it.

Like God, the Real for Lacanian thought is the unfathomable wedge of otherness at the heart of identity which makes us what we are, yet which—because it involves desire—also prevents us from being truly identical with ourselves. If psychoanalysis is a tragic vein of philosophy, it is among other things because this otherness at the core of our being, for which another name is desire, is as cruelly indifferent to our well-being as the Schopenhauerian Will. For Christian theology, this tragedy is resolved in principle in the life and death of Jesus, who is the 'son of God' in the sense that he is able to recognize himself in the demand and invitation of the Other. What he is for the Other (the Father) is what he is for himself. For us lesser mortals, it is a chronic uncertainty over whether we have indeed been recognized for what we are by the Other which sets in train desire. To declare in St John's words that Jesus and the Father are one is to claim that Jesus's dependence on the Other is not self-estrangement but self-fulfilment. At the core of his identity lies nothing but unconditional love. Even so, the son of God himself is not entirely exempt from that neurotic interrogation of the Other with which we non-divine creatures are afflicted. When Jesus cries out in despair on the cross, demanding of his Father why he has forsaken him, he appeals to an Other which has become momentarily inscrutable and Satanic. 'Am I doing the right thing? Why am I doing this at all?' is Jesus's anxious plea. He might well ask.

As we enter the epoch of modernity, the sublime is one name for the annihilating, regenerating power we have been investigating. A far more important name is freedom, as we shall see later. The sublime is any power which is perilous, shattering, ravishing, traumatic, excessive, exhilarating, dwarfing, astonishing, uncontainable, overwhelming, boundless, obscure, terrifying, enthralling, and uplifting. As such, like so many modern aesthetic concepts, it is among other things a secularized version of God. In modern times, art has been often enough forced to stand in for the Almighty. The sublime is a glimpse of infinity which dissolves our identity and shakes us to our roots, but in an agreeable kind of way. It warps the very inner structure of the mind, tugging us loose from the slackening grasp of reason. Like the divine and the Dionysian, it is enrapturing as well as devastating—which is to say that it is not hard to detect in it the shadowy presence of the death drive.

Like tragedy, the sublime allows us vicariously to indulge our fantasies of immortality, flouting our own finitude and playing a titillating 'can't catch me' game with death. To experience our destruction in art rather than reality is to live out a kind of virtual death, a sort of death-in-life. Confronted with the vista of raging oceans which cannot drown us because they are no more than pigment on canvas, we can know the delirious pleasures of defeating death (so that death itself comes cravenly to die), at the very moment that we can also feel free to embrace our own mortality. The sublime allows us to blend a joy in our own cartoon-like unkillability with the contrary pleasures of being decentred and dissolved. As such, it is both self-affirmative and self-destructive, and each in terms of the other. If we have passed symbolically through death yet are still breathing, death has been pressed into the service of eternal life.

The sublime thus involves a rhythm of death and resurrection, as we suffer a radical loss of identity only to have that selfhood more richly restored to us. These fearful powers blot us out into a kind of nothingness; yet like God this is a fertile rather than barren void, since to suffer the loss of all our distinguishing features is to be granted an epiphany of pure selfhood. Feeling crushed and oppressed thus turns at its nadir into its opposite. A vulnerable object becomes an infinite subject. By identifying ourselves with the boundlessness of the sublime, we cease to be anything in particular, but thereby become potentially everything. In this dazzling emptiness, all and nothing are closely allied, since both are absolved from limits. Enraptured by a consciousness of our own creative powers, in contrast to our physical pettiness, we come to recognize that true sublimity lies inside ourselves. In fact, it *is* ourselves. What appeared strange and dreadful is actually as close as breathing, while what seemed nearest to us—ourselves—is also what is most outlandish. Even to know the sublime only negatively, as an awed sense of our own paltriness, is already to be on terms with it. It is for this reason that feeling utterly inconsiderable can tip over into a sense of omnipotence. This fertile abyss into which we are plunged turns out to be nothing less than the human subject, which is as far beyond representation as infinity.

The shapeless immensity of the sublime is thus both friendly and foreign, under our skin yet a whole cosmos away. Like tragedy, it involves a rhythm of identity and difference. But there is also a manic-depressive oscillation about it, as we are pitched into abysmal ocean depths only to be snatched up triumphantly to the stars. If we can conquer our dread of the annihilating forces which seek to tear us apart, it is because they evoke an uncannily familiar echo at the very core of our subjectivity. In an ironic reversal, what was about to expunge us from existence ends up reinforcing a sense of our supreme value. It has even been suggested that this rhythm lies somewhere near the obscure origins of art and ritual. By identifying through the act of mimesis with the forces which endangered them, men and women sought to install something of that perilous power within themselves. Imitation is the sincerest form of appropriation.

St Augustine was perhaps the first major philosopher to see the self as a kind of abyss or infinity. For him, it is sublime in its unfathomable depths, and nothing is more dizzying than the movement by which the mind tries fruitlessly to grasp hold of itself. The true terror at the heart of reality is the human subject, which for Augustine is a kind of nothingness. Fearful of this gulf in being, the fundamentalist seeks to stuff it with absolute values and unbending principles. In doing so, he risks unleashing a different kind of terror.

If the sublime confers on us a pleasurable sense of imperishability, it also allows us to perform our own deaths vicariously, thus mastering our dread of them in that dummy run known as art. By making our destiny our decision, converting our fate into our choice, we are able to pluck life from death and freedom from necessity. If tragedy is an early example of this enjoyably masochistic art-form, a later one is the horror movie, which by 'virtualizing' distress also mixes pain and pleasure. We delight in vampires as long as they are not busy sinking their teeth into our necks. Among the real-life equivalents of this virtuality is *Schadenfreude*, in which we revel sadistically in the calamities of others. A character in August Strindberg's *Dream Play* remarks with brutal candour that people have an instinctive horror of others' good fortune, while Dostoevsky writes in *Crime and Punishment* of 'that strange inward glow of satisfaction which we experience when disaster strikes our neighbour, however sincere our pity and sympathy' (Part 2, ch. 7). The latter reservation is vital: as in tragedy or the sublime, we feel both pity *and* pleasure. Nietzsche, as usual, presses the matter a stage further: to see others suffer, he gleefully suggests in *The Genealogy of Morals*, is a joy inferior only to making them suffer.

When terror ceases to be second-hand, however, it quickly sheds its allure, as Edmund Burke was not slow to see. 'When danger and pain press too nearly,' he observes in his *Philosophical Enquiry into the Origin of our Ideas of the Sublime and Beautiful*, 'they are incapable of giving any delight, and are simply terrible.' Antigone is sublime, but a bomb in a crowded bus station is not. As that other great theorist of the sublime, Immanuel Kant, comments in his *Critique of Judgement*, 'it is impossible to find satisfaction in terror that is seriously felt'. For Kant, sublime eruptions like the French Revolution could be admired as long as they were aestheticized, contemplated from a secure distance. There are times when the terror which the symbolic order has safely defused, sublimating it into the majesty of law and sovereignty, comes bursting through the fault lines of that order in the shape of the ineffable Real. It is this which we know among other things as terrorism, a fury which is unleashed not least when the law has fallen into disrepute. Yet it is also a built-in possibility, a disaster waiting to happen.

Then, as in psychosis, the boundaries between fantasy and reality begin to blur, as the Real stages an impossible appearance in reality itself. Raw and implacable, what was contained through sublimation returns to wreak its vindictive wrath on the innocent. This is not a sublimity which both appals and seduces. Instead, the responses of pity and fear are wrenched apart, as we direct the former to the victims and the latter to the perpetrators. In Aristotle's view, tragedy is a form of social therapy: by allowing us to indulge certain politically disruptive emotions, it drains off this dangerous surplus and in doing so strengthens the state. With terrorism, exactly the opposite occurs, as in a frightful process of desublimation the horrors of the tragic and the sublime invade everyday life itself.

For Edmund Burke, the law itself is an image of sublimity, since it must blend terror and kindliness, coercion and consent, in well-calculated proportion.[1] As René Girard remarks of such sovereign power: 'Like Oedipus, the king is at once stranger and son, the most intimate of insiders and the most bizarre of outsiders; he is an exemplar of enormous tenderness and frightful savagery.'[2] If the law is terrible to look upon, it also wins our affectionate compliance. Like David Hume, who held rather surprisingly that the governed always had the upper hand in the end when it came to power, Burke is convinced that all authority rests finally on love, sympathy, and free assent. We do not revere a power which is too ferocious, nor are we impressed by the kind of law which simply tells us where we have gone wrong. We may be cowed by such a code, but we do not love it. This view has political implications. The surest way to grapple the colonies to the Crown, in Burke's view, is to secure their affections. Long before Antonio Gramsci, Burke, himself a colonial subject transplanted to the metropolis, had grasped the meaning of hegemony. It was this, in Burke's view, that had broken down so disastrously in India, Ireland, and America.

Fear of the law is more likely to breed rebels than docile citizens. To succeed, a jurisdiction must win not just our respect but our veneration. But neither do we revere a power which is too obsequious and ingratiating. We must identify with the law, discovering in it an imaginary image of ourselves; yet we must also be suitably daunted by its grandeur, stunned into a submissive sense of our own negligibility. This linchpin of the symbolic order must foster an imaginary identity on our part, but it also must have a minatory whiff of the Real about it. If an effective sovereignty must hail us like old cronies, it must also be aloofly even-handed, turning its back haughtily on the lot of us.

These are not incompatible requirements, since Burke recognizes that to be intimidated is by no means entirely disagreeable. He is one of our earliest theorists of sado-masochism. What makes the law so potent is just the fact that we relish being browbeaten. It is masochism which keeps the social order from collapsing, as we enjoy being relieved of our guilt by punishment. Yet it is the law which stokes our guilt in the first place; and the more grisly relish we take in its sanctions, the more guilt-ridden we become. Authority daunts and delights us at the same time—though Burke believes that the pleasures of being in love with the law outweigh our yearning to be petrified by it. He is not, in short, a Machiavellian. We are more likely to submit to authority because it solicits our loyalties than because it threatens to hang us by the neck.

The law for Burke is masculine, and he knew enough of the gibbet from his Irish background not to underestimate its horrors.[3] Its high-handed ukases risk traumatizing us into gibbering wrecks, which is scarcely the best way to produce compliant citizens. Unrestrained terror on the part of the state, Burke considered, would provoke rather than pacify rebellion. It is not a warning much heeded today. This masculine law is the law as terrorist, unleashing upon us a sadistic aggression madly in excess of our faults. It is the law as Satan and superego, before which we can never be justified. This law thrives on our frailties, since without these misdemeanours it would be out of business; but it does not accept them. That is the prerogative of love. So the law, for the Burke of the aesthetic treatise, must turn transvestite, decking itself out in female drapery to conceal its unlovely phallus. It must be sweetened and tempered, so as to be modulated into what we might now call hegemony.

In Burke's view, women are beautiful whereas men are sublime; and only an epicene power which combines both aesthetic dimensions will prove effective. The law must coerce like a man but cajole like a woman, chastise like a father but indulge us like a mother. In his treatise on aesthetics, Burke rather quaintly proposes the figure of the grandfather as combining masculine strength with feminine tenderness. The law, then, is necessarily self-divided, as Slavoj Žižek notes: 'One can say that the law divides itself necessarily into an "appeasing" law and a "mad" law: the opposition between the law and its transgressions repeats itself inside . . . the law itself.'[4] It must be a cross-dresser, concealing its true gender. Yet there is always an ugly bulge in its alluring garments.

Since the destruction of the World Trade Center, the ugly bulge beneath the West's democratic garments has been embarrassingly on show. While some Western leaders have been shamelessly stripping power of its veils of consensus and moral rectitude, one or two others have sought to cover this nakedness with various rather tattered fig-leaves of legality, lest sovereignty itself fall permanently into discredit. The more Western society reacts to terrorist assault with an answerable illegality, the more it depletes the very spiritual and political resources which it takes itself to be protecting. Which is no doubt part of what terrorism has in mind. In this sense, triumph becomes failure, as military victory upends itself into moral defeat. We shall see later a similar inversion of victory and defeat in the case of the terrorists themselves.

A certain fury, then, lies at the heart of society, and can always burst destructively out again. Burke speaks in his reflections on the French Revolution of the English Constitution as 'temper[ing] with an aweful [sic] gravity . . . the spirit of freedom, leading in itself to misrule and excess'. Freedom itself always has something anarchic and excessive about it. It is only law and order which can restrain it. Yet an externally imposed order is never the most authoritative. Worst of all, the law itself is simply a sublimated version of the very violence and terror which it seeks to contain. It draws its force from these very obstreperous energies, rather as for Freud the superego has its roots sunk deep in the id and would not be effective if it had not.

The law must not be seen naked, or it will shed its authority along with its garments. This in Burke's view is the real crime of the French Jacobins—that they have ripped the comely veils of hegemony from the law and exposed its phallic barbarism for all to see. What is wrong with the Revolution is not just its butchery and despotism, but the fact that it has let the ideological cat out of the bag. In discrediting themselves, the French have helped to expose the clay feet of authority in general, which now stands exposed as the terrorist it secretly is. 'All the decent drapery of life,' Burke protests of the Jacobin Terror, 'is to be rudely torn off.'[5] The revolutionaries have stripped the law of its age-old mystique and turned the pitiless searchlight of reason on its shyly veiled origins. They have delved indecently into these secret places, uncovering the primal scene and dragging into daylight what should be at all costs concealed.

Yet this remorseless light of reason dazzles to the point of blindness. Those such as Oedipus or the Jacobins who probe too closely into these shameful mysteries will be struck sightless in punishment for their hubris. In the case of the Jacobins, this blindness is known as political dogmatism. It is their own excessively luminous reason which puts out their eyes. The origins of power are sublime, beyond all representation. For Burke, there is a bad sublime as well as a good one, and the distance between them is as wide as the English Channel. Yet the distinction is not as clear as it might seem, since the destructive species of the sublime which is on the rampage in Paris is a desublimated version of what remains a politically indispensable force. Rather as fire drives out fire, so all that will banish the bad sublime is the good one. And this is not good news for Burke's day, as it is not for our own.

This is to say that Burke is not averse to a touch of terror from time to time. There are occasions when the law needs to expose its phallus. Burke thinks that we need a therapeutic dose of terror every now and then, to prevent society from growing enervated and effete. Machiavelli believed much the same. The most desirable political condition, so Burke considers in his aesthetic treatise, is one of 'tranquillity tinged with terror'. Or, in an alternative coding, a mixture of the Apollinian and the Dionysian. Too pitiless a law will leave us in the state of mind which contemporary terrorists aim to create: speechless, paralytic, unable to feel or think. The survivors of terrorist assaults are images of the living dead.[6] They are not the sort of deferential but resourceful citizens which Burke wants to see. Yet if we are not to become bovine and inert, we need, in Burke's own term, a judicious 'stiffening' of the sublime. Terror of a sort must live on within the 'feminine' sedateness and docility of everyday social life, as the Furies live on as honoured guests within the Athenian *polis*.

The sublime, in other words, must inscribe itself within the beautiful; and one form which this takes in Burke's view is labour. Labour has the mingled pain and pleasure of the sublime. There is something about production which is both gratifying and coercive. In Euripides's phrase, it is a 'sweet toil'. What remains sublime about this social order, then, is its dynamic enterprise. A strain of virile strenuousness lingers on in polite bourgeois society in the sublimated guise of rivalry and entrepreneurship. It is to be found for Burke in all daring, heroic enterprises, which are sublime in the sense that they involve both pain and pleasure, fear and fulfilment. Sublimity is a question of climbing mountains, not just contemplating them. In Marxist terms, one might venture the formulation that for Burke the economic base is Dionysian, while the civic super-structure is Apollinian. To prevent humanity from lapsing into torpid complacency, so he argues in his aesthetic treatise, God has planted in us a sense of ambition and competition. The sublime is the antisocial condition of sociality, the lawless masculine force which violates the feminine enclosure of polite society, but which in doing so regenerates it. It plays something like the role which Dionysus wishes to perform in Pentheus's Thebes.

The truly terrible sublime, however, is the lawless revolt which established the political order in the first place—one which is thankfully almost lost to memory in England, but which the outraged Burke can now observe taking place across the Channel. Yet the contrast between a law-abiding England and a revolutionary France is in one sense deceptive. For established political society sublimates the terror which originally went into its making; and the name of this displaced ferocity is law and order. In an unpalatable irony, then, it is sovereignty itself which is closest to the tumult of society's lawless beginnings. The law is the place where the revolutionary wrath which brought society to birth finally takes up its home. Like Oedipus, then, it is sovereign and outlaw together. The forces which overthrew a previous form of life are now dedicated to the defence of a new one. The Furies are enshrined at the heart of the city. The criminal has become the cop.

This is not to suggest that the law is simply a form of terrorism, in some naive libertarian wisdom. It is infantile ultra-leftism which imagines that all law is oppressive, all authority obnoxious. Only those with no need of the law's protection can afford to be so cavalier. They forget that the law can be a shield for the powerless as well as a weapon of the privileged. Those for whom power is always a negative term are generally those who have no pressing need for it.[7] It is the dispossessed who need power to change their situation, and the well-heeled liberal who can afford to be contemptuous of the stuff. Power's attempts to subjugate the world should surely win our applause as well as provoke our condemnation. It is necessary for us to pull rank over Nature by building sea defences and irrigating deserts. The problem is not that power is repugnant, but that there is an excessive, gratuitous strain within it which can always get out of hand, some built-in perversity which delights in dominion for its own sake. This is the unreason implicit in even reasonable forms of power. There is madness in its method. Besides, insanity can be a surfeit of reason, not just a shortage of it. It was Freud who commented that the nearest thing to philosophy was paranoia. When reason is pressed beyond all rational bounds, it flips over into madness; and one name for this lunacy for Burke was the Jacobin Terror. The unreason at the core of reason is now on the loose in the streets of Paris, and nobody can look on this unfathomable fury and live.

Middle-class society, then, requires a salutary stiffening of the sublime. Capitalism, for example, needs the sublime phenomena of risk and danger in order to operate, however much it might strive to copper-bottom its enterprises. It is a daredevil, free-booting form of life, but one perpetually at peril of being stifled by its own sedate manners and civil society, which is what Burke calls 'beauty'. It is by being threatened by competition that the entrepreneur springs most vigorously into life, and this for Burke is a minor image of sublimity. Whole technologies of knowledge are harnessed to the business of rendering capitalism's profits as safe and predictable as possible; yet if the system could really calculate its outcomes with absolute precision, we would no longer be speaking of freedom, and the whole operation would prove to be self-cancelling. This is why in the film *Minority Report*, the temptation to pre-calculate the future must finally be relinquished as a threat to the very freedom it seeks to secure. Freedom is by definition open-ended, and so must submit to being fearful, perilous, and half-blind.

Danger, as Burke sees, is an integral part of this social order (indeed, it is dangerous to be without it), which is why it can never entirely purge itself of the sublime. Death is a condition of life. Politically speaking, the consummation of this in modern times is fascism, for which the ideal social order is one which combines both conditions. Fascism dreams of a capitalism which is both infinitely dynamic and absolutely regulated—one whose energies are vital and spontaneous, yet which is at the same time as eternal and immutable as death itself. It is a reminder that only Romantics and business executives use the word 'dynamic' as unequivocally positive.

Too much serenity, then, can sink society without trace. When modern states have lived down their disorderly origins and settled into civic respectability, this very tranquillity may trigger such disorder once again. One of the many causes of political terrorism lies in the bland gentrification of conventional politics. The less the orthodox political sphere seems responsive to the demands of those it excludes, the more those demands can assume a pathological form, blowing apart the very public arena in which they had previously sought a hearing. Terrorism is among other things a reaction to a politics which has grown vacuously managerial. This non-political species of politics, emptied as it is of so many momentous questions, then finds itself confronted by a brand of politics which is equally disdainful of the conventionally political. The defusing of politics is countered by the denial of it, as too little passion yields ground to a monstrous excess of it.

Both conventional and terrorist kinds of politics are in their different ways politics of the gesture. In the case of political terror, this gesture takes the form of a disruptive Surrealist 'happening', one which outdoes the Surrealists in aiming to shatter bodies as well as minds. At the root of your so-called reason, so terror proclaims to orthodox political society, lies the ravenous unreason of greed, power, and exploitation, none of which can be rationally justified. Reason is founded in what outflanks it. And this so-called rationality deploys an ungovernable violence in its defence. In rejecting a rational politics altogether, we shall expose the violence at the root of your supposed civility. All that is missing here is the recognition that to pile innocent bodies knee-deep around your enemy is not to refute him.

Burke's thoughts about the sublime touch on a contradiction endemic to the middle-class social order. It is a community wedded to peace and legality, hierarchy and civility, as the necessary conditions for its strenuous enterprise. An individualist society needs an especially well-founded state if it is not to fragment and fall apart. A barbarous, swashbuckling aristocracy thus gives way to a dull yet decent bourgeoisie. Yet the Apollinian and the Dionysian are not so easily reconciled, as the anarchic energies of market society threaten to burst through the stable frames of legality and morality which support them. Peace makes for war: the more settled conditions allow market forces to flourish, the more instability at home and antagonism abroad they are likely to breed. In this sense, bourgeois societies are continually at risk of undermining the very values which legitimate them. The stout burgher is simply the lawless entrepreneur at home or at prayer. The angelic and the demonic are facets of the same social world.

This is no doubt one reason why English literature, offspring of the longest-established middle-class nation in history, returns again and again to the secret complicity between the criminal and the capitalist. If the honest bourgeois detests the bohemian and the iconoclast, it is partly because he has more in common with them than he cares to admit. The reverse is also true. Daniel Defoe's Moll Flanders may be a thief and a whore, but she plies her trade as hard-headedly as any banker. If business types can be brigands, outlaws can be tediously suburban. John Gay's *The Beggar's Opera* introduces us to pimps and con-men conducting a well-organized business. Mr Merdle, the master financier of Dickens's *Little Dorrit*, turns out to be a cheap crook. Pip, the socially aspiring hero of *Great Expectations*, is living unknown to himself on the proceeds of violent crime. Mr Verloc of Joseph Conrad's *The Secret Agent* is both a small shopkeeper and an underground political *provocateur* responsible for the slaughter of his mentally defective stepson. As Bertolt Brecht once enquired: what's robbing a bank compared to founding one? Balzac's flamboyant Vautrin in fact manages to combine both roles, as a master criminal who also acts as the trusted banker of his underworld colleagues.

It is no wonder, then, that a Jekyll-and-Hyde or Holmes-and-Moriarty doubleness persists through the literature of modernity. In England, this paradox of an illicit or revolutionary order is apparent as early as John Milton's Satan, pompous princeling and fiery rebel. The middle class tend to project their own dangerous or disruptive qualities on to some monstrous other, who shadows them as Mephistopheles shadows Faust; but the trouble with this solution from a literary viewpoint is that it leaves the devil with all the best tunes. By disavowing one's more diabolical aspects and projecting them elsewhere, virtue is in danger of becoming tedious and insipid. Like some quaint Edwardian bicycle, it is admirable to behold, but it will not get you anywhere. It is when the good appear bland and bloodless that the bad take on a beguiling panache. 'Wicked' becomes a term of commendation.

The situation is made more acute by the fact that middle-class civilization tends to define virtue not in Aristoteleian or Thomist terms of vital capacity and pleasurable self-fulfilment, but in terms of moral habits which are a good deal harder to make dramatically appealing: thrift, prudence, chastity, meekness, abstinence, frugality, obedience, dutifulness, self-discipline, and the like. Bourgeois morality spells the death of the imagination, which is one reason why art in this epoch comes to seem inherently transgressive. The whole point of the imagination is to range beyond the given, so that novels like Samuel Richardson's *Clarissa* and Jane Austen's *Mansfield Park*, which affirm the more decorous, acquiescent virtues, seem curiously self-undoing. Austen in particular is ironically aware of how unavoidably unglamorous moral goodness is. If Richardson were really at one with his saintly heroine Clarissa, he could not have written the novel, a project which involves feeling his way imaginatively into the libertine Lovelace as well. Yet unless evil is made compellingly real, the virtue which resists it is drained of value.

What we find in modern writing, then, is a series of coupled characters who are both strangers and kinsfolk; and this coupling is a sign of the rivalry-cum-affinity between burgher and bohemian, citizen and criminal, law and trespass. Each term conjures up the other: a static, lifeless moral code breeds its lawless opposite as surely as Oliver Twist gives rise to Fagin, or Little Nell to the malignant Quilp. One thinks of Othello and Iago, the God and Satan of *Paradise Lost*, Clarissa and Lovelace, Blake's Urizen and Los, Goethe's Faust and Mephistopheles, Nelly Dean and Heathcliff, Ahab and Moby-Dick, Alyosha and Ivan Karamazov, Leopold Bloom and Stephen Dedalus, Zeitblom and Leverkühn of Thomas Mann's *Doctor Faustus*. In several of these twinnings, it is impossible to decide whether the partners are allies or adversaries, as Franco Moretti remarks of Faust and Mephisopheles.[8]

Or if not impossible, then at least instructively difficult. In most of these cases, a principle which is virtuous but imaginatively restricted confronts a destructive yet life-giving force with which it betrays a covert affinity. Other instances weave more complex variants on this opposition. Milton's Satan is a fallen angel, Iago is perversely fascinated by Othello, Clarissa and her seducer Lovelace are probably in love. The restlessly kinetic Dedalus glimpses a surrogate father in the spiritually static Bloom. The stolidly bourgeois Zeitblom enjoys the kind of horrified intimacy with the diabolical Leverkühn that liberal capitalism has with fascism. A parallel ambiguity marks some of the protagonists of the later Henry James, who may be read as either angelic or demonic, saints or schemers.

If the lawgiver is also in a sense the wrongdoer, it is among other things because most law-abiding regimes were first established by conquest, revolution, invasion, or usurpation. As the Irish dramatist Denis Johnston remarks: 'No nation is an immaculate conception.' The transgression was there from the beginning. The snake was curled up in Eden from the outset. How, indeed, could there be law without it? And how can God's mercy be made manifest unless we are intent on sinning against him? Perhaps it was when we realized that the Creator was furtively egging the serpent on (since without the Fall, no redemption) that we needed to reach for our fig leaves. Most social orders have contaminated origins, but this is a particular embarrassment to those which, like middle-class ones, cling to the virtues of a quiet life. The middle class wants not revolutionary turmoil but perpetual peace, so that it can shake down to the sober, unglamorous business of money-making and family-building. Like the child of Freud's family romance syndrome, it seeks to disavow its discreditable origins and dream up a more prestigious provenance.

Yet the profit motive and military aggression are in fact closely allied; and constructing a peaceable middle-class order in the first place usually involves upheaval and illegality. The coming of law and order was neither lawful nor orderly. There is not much that the founders of nations need to be told about original sin. How then can the middle class square its moral idealism with its bloodstained beginnings? The problem, in fact, is that the violence of middle-class society is not simply a question of its origins: it lives on within it in the form of competition, exploitation, military conquest, and disruptive individualism. Revolution is still with us, and its name is the status quo. This social order must square its drive for stability with the fact that, uniquely among historical regimes, its revolution never ends—that capitalism, as Marx reminds us, is an inherently transgressive force, perpetually agitating, unmasking, disrupting, and dissolving. As far as dynamism and stasis are concerned, then, the bourgeoisie land themselves with the worst of both worlds: an unending revolution linked to a uniquely pressing need for stability.

In some tribal communities, so the anthropologists tell us, the chief-elect must commit a number of real or symbolic trespasses before he is confirmed in office. Today's fast-living heirs to thrones have no problem with this requirement. Middle-class governance has its initial trespasses too; but this traumatic convulsion at the source of the social order has then to be lived down, if society is to persuade itself that a staid but secure existence is preferable to an exciting but volatile one. It must also be lived down if it is not to serve as a reminder to the middle class's political opponents that revolutionary change is always on the agenda. If they did it, so can their antagonists. One of the more minor perils of making revolutions is that you draw the attention of your adversaries to the inherent plasticity of the world, which was not quite what you intended.

For Hegel, as we shall see later, this built-in contradiction between order and anarchy can be resolved by being cast in narrative form. First there was the wild liberty of the middle class's insurrectionary phase; but later on society sobers up, recovers from its revolutionary hangover, and exercises its freedom more responsibly. Yet Hegel, as we shall see, is aware that we are speaking here of two permanent dimensions of bourgeois freedom, not just of two historical phases. The traumatic effects of repressing an original revolutionary violence will never be entirely erased; instead, they will break out again from time to time in the form of social neurosis or political terror.

The middle classes, then, must make the transition from bandits to bankers—a precarious shift, to be sure, since there is something inherently anti-social about the kind of freedom they promote. Where they were once heroes, they are now accountants. Epic drama gives way to sober realism. A swash-buckling cast of warriors yields to a colourless battalion of clerks. As Marx enquired, what becomes of heroic mythology in the age of railways, locomotives, and electric telegraphs?[9] In France, the high revolutionary politics of Stendhal yield to the mundane realism of Balzac and Flaubert. In England, the radical Blake, Byron, and Shelley are shouldered aside by Tennyson and Trollope. Like a hippie applying to law school, the new bourgeois order must draw a veil of oblivion over its ignominious beginnings. When Marxists admiringly draw attention to these revolutionary origins, the middle classes themselves tend to squirm with the mortification of those whose naughty antics as children are fondly recalled by their doting parents. Beginnings are an embarrassment to those in the grip of exotic fantasies of self-invention—which is to say, the hard-boiled pragmatists who persuade themselves that they have no parentage, since the way things are now is essentially how they have always been.

It is not hard to find the traces of this shift from epic to realism in literature. Indeed, one name for it is the novel.[10] Walter Scott's historical fiction actually takes this transition as a central part of its subject-matter, combining the romance of a dying clan culture in the Jacobite Highlands with the progressive yet prosaic social order of the Hanoverian Lowlands. In Scott, the conflict-cum-alliance between bandits and bankers assumes an arrestingly literal form, as romance and realism are interwoven to create a new, formidably influential literary genre. Romance trades in the marvellous and trangressive, and realism in the mundane; so that by forging a complex unity out of these two literary modes, Scott can fashion a form of writing which is true at once to the revolutionary origins and the quotidian life of the early bourgeois epoch. It was his good fortune as an author to be born into a society in which these two formations coexisted spatially, as Highlands and Lowlands, rather than simply as distinct historical phases.

It is such distinct phases, however, that we find in Stendhal, for whose high-minded heroes what matters is the conflict between the revolutionary idealism of the Napoleonic past and the degraded power-politics of the present. For Scott, the loss of an epic past is ambiguously welcome, whereas for Stendhal it is unequivocally tragic. Battles and executions, Stendhal laments, had given way to a world of taxes and statistics.[11] Power and idealism are no longer compatible. Even so, his fiction marks one of the last points at which politics, with its courtly intrigues, scheming Jesuits, glamorous secret agents, and military valour, can still furnish the stuff of romance. By the time of Flaubert's *Sentimental Education*, political revolution and everyday life intersect only contingently, in ways which devalue them both.

If Stendhal finds heroism in politics, Balzac unearths it in economics—in the protean, larger-than-life creatures of post-revolutionary society, with their bottomless rapacity, prodigious vitality, unslakeable ambitions, exorbitant appetites, and tragic capacity for self-destruction. High drama can still be wrought from a world of bankers and charlatans, louche entrepreneurs and scheming social upstarts. These monstrous personalities are still close enough to the wellsprings of bourgeois revolution to stand forth as epic creations. In an astonishing irony, the traditional stuff of melodrama, mythology, and romance can now be extracted from that lowly, unpromising material known as finance and commerce. The aristocratic warriors of Homer and Virgil have yielded ground to the mega-stars of the moneyed classes, with their predatory instincts and death-dealing obsessions.

Stendhal laments the fading of heroic glory from the middle-class domain; but Balzac, by turning his attention to *capitalist* rather than *bourgeois* society, to the sublime rather than the beautiful, recognizes that this heroism has simply changed address. All those epic conflicts and rumbustious energies are now to be discovered exactly where earlier writers would never have been able to look for them—in the melodrama of property and inheritance, the thrills and spills of the marriage market and stock exchange, in wolfish competitors and rapscallion opportunists. The dynamism of this social order lies in its material base, not in its social or political superstructure. Sublimity lives on in men whose wealth beggars the imagination. Tragedy suvives in the fate of the swindled and exploited. As the narrator of *Lost Illusions* comments, 'the anguish caused by poverty is no less worthy of attention than the crises which turn life upside-down for the mighty and privileged persons of this earth' (Part 2, ch. 1). It is a new democracy of destitution.

By the time of Joyce's *Ulysses*, bourgeois epic will have become mock-epic—though in the meanwhile Émile Zola's *Au Bonheur des Dames* manages to pluck a final piece of heroic mythology from nineteenth-century capitalism. It does so by turning from the dull compulsion of the world of production, of *Germinal* and *La Terre*, to the emergent sphere of large-scale consumerism, with its eroticized, palatial department stores and carnival of sensual delights. This is a necessary displacement, since in the wake of Balzac and Dickens, the literature of middle-class modernity finds it hard to represent the very material forces to which it owes its existence. This is largely because these forces now seem too sordid and ignoble for imaginative portrayal. There are notable exceptions such as Thomas Mann's *Buddenbrooks*; but this is the narrative of a cultivated, haut-bourgeois mercantile class rather than one of jobbers and brokers.

In general, it seems that the literature of modernity can depict an entrepreneur only by painting him as something else: as desert-island castaway (Robinson Crusoe), philosopher-mage (Goethe's Faust), dashing aristocrat (Disraeli), Amazonian heroine (Charlotte Bronte's Shirley), self-tormenting tragic protagonist (Melville's Ahab), or stage villain (Dickens's Dombey or Bounderby). There is also the industrialist as intellectual: Charles Gould of Conrad's *Nostromo*, Arnheim of Robert Musil's *The Man Without Qualities*, or Gerald Crich of D. H. Lawrence's *Women in Love*. In none of these cases is the character observed doing any work. It is now, ironically, the realm of production which seems to have been privatized. We do not see inside these men's mines and factories in any detail, any more than we see anyone at work on Jane Austen's landed estates.

In Henry James's *The Ambassadors*, we are carefully not told what it is that the Newsome family manufactures. A handful of Virginia Woolf's characters may be something in the City, but exactly what is as much a mystery to the reader as it appears to be to the author. The material powers which give birth to modernity slip into its fiction only in cloaked and muffled form. Literature is the kind of commerce which is ignorant of itself. To represent merchants and manufacturers, it often enough finds itself reaching back to more traditional forms (myth, pastoral, melodrama, romance), or transplanting the protagonist from his office or factory to some more exotic, elemental setting such as Conrad's jungle or Melville's ocean.

We may return, after this literary diversion, to the need to live down one's disreputable origins. Can it be that social harmony is simply a forgetfulness of an unruly past? Are law and order ultimately a question of amnesia? These are no wild leftist proposals, but the common currency of a conservative style of thought. David Hume, perhaps the greatest of British philosophers, cautions that if we investigate the origins of nations, we shall find there rebellion and usurpation. 'Time alone,' he declares, 'gives solidity to (the rulers') right; and operating gradually on the minds of men, reconciles them to any authority, and makes it seem just and reasonable.'[12] The older you are as a nation, the more respectable you become, as long-buried crimes come to grow on you like old cronies. Political power is founded on fading memory. Oblivion, as Dionysus knew, is the performance-enhancing drug which allows civilizations to work effectively. In Schiller's drama *Wallenstein*, the hero observes that 'The march of years has power to sanctify; | Whatever's grey with age, men will call holy. | Once in possession, you are in the right' (Act 1, Scene 4). 'Time,' writes Burke, 'has, by degrees . . . blended and coalited the conquered with the conquerors.'[13] As an Irishman, this champion of the English constitution was well aware of just how little this was true of his own exploited nation. This was one reason why he adopted another, in which the tainted springs of power were old enough to be shrouded in mystery.

Blaise Pascal is quite as candid as Hume on the need to obliterate one's genesis. 'The truth about the (original) usurpation,' he writes conspiratorially, 'must not be made apparent: it came about originally without reason and has become reasonable. We must see that it is regarded as authentic and eternal, and its origins must be hidden if we do not want it soon to end.'[14] It is a far cry from the pious doctrine that the social order is the upshot of God's will—a doctrine designed for the masses rather than the intelligentsia. The law for Pascal is not revered because it is sacred, but sacred because it is revered. The populace, he comments, think that laws exist because they are just, whereas the truth is the other way round: it is force which creates opinion and determines what is right. Coercion gives birth to consent.

This was not a view shared by Immanuel Kant. But he, too, considered speculations on the sources of political power to be a menace to the state.[15] The plain-minded Montaigne likewise scoffed at such abstruse enquiries. The modern French philosopher Joseph de Maistre agreed with Pascal that the violence at the foundation of the state must at all costs be concealed; he, too, held that political power survived only as long as its origins were cloaked in mystery. Ernest Renan observed that a nation is defined as much by what it forgets as by what it remembers. Friedrich Nietzsche writes in a similar vein: 'Cheerfulness, the good conscience, the joyful deed, confidence in the future—all of them depend, in the case of an individual as of a nation, on the existence of a dark line dividing the bright and discernible from the unilluminable and dark; on one's being just as able to forget at the right time as to remember at the right time . . .'[16]

How successful middle-class society is in living down its disreputable past varies from place to place. In England, owing to the mediated, protracted process by which the middle classes came to power, it was possible to claim that there had been no decisive rupture. There could not be an outfit known as the Daughters of the English Revolution, as there is an unsavoury such equivalent in the United States, since the English revolution is deemed not to have taken place. It would be as absurd an institution as the Sons of Saudi Democracy. The English had managed to pull off the most successful revolution of all—the kind which nobody remembered ever having taken place. Yet the price which they paid for this apparent continuity was a high one. If American capitalism was too frenetic, the English version was too hidebound. The one suffered from a surplus of energy, and the other from an excess of order.

In the United States, bourgeois revolution took an honourably anti-colonial form, one to be celebrated rather than disavowed. The brash explicitness of American capitalism remains true in spirit to the revolutionary cataclysm which brought it to birth— one which is anyway too recent to live down. Insurrection lives on in the form of restless innovation and robust enterprise. The pioneer spirit was displaced rather than dissolved. The epic rapacity which subdued the land in the first place carried on as regular business. Probably no other people on earth use the word 'aggressive' in such a positive fashion, and no group outside psychoanalytic circles is so fond of the word 'dream'. Having no aristocracy to co-opt or decapitate, the United States had to hand no ready-made heritage of hierarchy and stability, which is one of several reasons why its brand of capitalism was more visibly lawless. Unlike its former proprietors, it could not swathe the unlovely aggression of the marketplace in the decorous garments of gentility. Perhaps this is one of several reasons why the Supreme Being has bulked so large there—why one of the most materialist societies on earth is also one of the most portentously metaphysical. If there is little of Burke's tradition and time-hallowed custom to provide a basis for social stability, the Almighty can be drafted in instead. Law and order come to take up their abode within each citizen, in the shape of a high puritan conscience.

States which find it hard to live down their tumultuous beginnings because they are too raw and recent are likely to rank among the most unstable. Israel and Northern Ireland may serve as examples. It is hard to pass off your sovereignty as natural when everyone remembers their grandparents being pitched off their land. What is vital here, as Burke argues in his celebrated doctrine of prescription, is the sheer passage of time, which is enough to convert rebels into real estate agents. Legitimacy is really longevity. After a while, the revolutionaries who laid the basis of social order come to be seen as the enemies of it, as has happened in Ireland among other places, and history is revised accordingly. When society's conditions of possibility become its potential undoing, the gentrification of the revolution is complete.

The sublime, like the tragic or the Dionysian, is an attempt to think through a series of paradoxes—of victory and failure, infinity and mortality, order and anarchy, self-affirmation and self-dispossession—which lie at the heart of Western thought. Yet there is a sense in which all of these come to a head in the phenomenon which Burke describes as 'leading in itself to misrule and excess', and to whose extraordinary ambivalences we can now turn.

3

Fear and Freedom

FOR the modern age, the most sublime phenomenon of all is freedom, which like the god Dionysus is both angel and demon, beauty and terror. If there is something sacred about liberty it is not only because it is precious, but because it can destroy as well as create. In answer to the query 'Where does freedom come from?' modernity has tended to reply: 'From itself'. If freedom is to be an absolute value, then it must go all the way down and be founded in nothing but its own infinite plenitude. Otherwise, if we can point to a ground or prop which supports this freedom from the outside, it is struck instantly relative. 'Freedom,' writes Friedrich Schelling, 'is the one principle on which everything is supported.'[1] Yet to claim that a thing is grounded in itself is both a way of trumping those who question it, and a feeble tautology. It seems perilously close to confessing that it has no foundation at all—that humanity is standing simply on itself, which scarcely sounds the most solid of bases. Liberty is left hanging in a void, to act as its own origin, end, and legitimation. This is one reason why the modern age finds a tangible image of freedom in the work of art, which is likewise seen as self-grounded and autotelic.

In the pre-modern period, God had provided a solution of sorts to this dilemma. He was the answer to the question of where our freedom came from, in the sense that we became the free individuals we were by sharing in his own boundless liberty. This participation was traditionally known as grace. To claim that God made us in his own image and likeness was to say that where we were most like him was in our autonomy. There could be no graven images of Yahweh, since the only authentic image of him was human beings. Like him, too, we existed simply for the sake of it, as self-delighting, self-determining beings, rather than as functional parts of some greater totality. There was no more point to us than there was to God. It was by being dependent on him that we came into our own. God was not what stopped us from being ourselves, but the unsearchable power at the core of the self which allowed us to be what we were. To fall out of his hands was to lapse into nothingness. He was the ground of our freedom, not the obstacle to it. Being a 'creature' of the Almighty meant being dependent on his life for our own, and the life of God was nothing but freedom. This kind of dependency was therefore the reverse of slavery, as St Paul is eager to point out. Where we were most self-determining, there we were most truly his.

Freedom, then, could have the firmest possible foundation while still being unconstrained. And this seemed to resolve an awkward problem. For as soon as we think of a firm foundation, we can always imagine slipping another one beneath it. To think of such a ground is to think of it as a finite object, and thus to deny its foundational nature—rather as Ludwig Wittgenstein once remarked that it is hard to imagine an origin without feeling that one could always go back beyond it. If God was our ground, however, this ceased to be such a conundrum. For God was clearly not any kind of object or finite principle, and thus seemed to provide just the sort of foundation we wanted, namely one which went all the way down. Nothing could go further down than God, who was a bottomless abyss of being. To take your stand on him (provided you could momentarily shelve the query 'all the way down to *what*?') was thus to take your stand on infinity. Because this ground of our being con-sisted of pure freedom, we could be securely anchored while still feeling as though we were walking on air.

If God was anywhere, then, he had to be lurking in the inner sanctum of human subjectivity, since it was this which appeared most infinite about us. Subjectivity goes on forever in every direction: I can contemplate the vision of my origin or my end, but it is still I who am doing the contemplating. I cannot shuck off my subjectivity any more than I can leap out of my body. This is why self-consciousness for Schelling is a source of light which 'shines only forward, not backward'.[2] The subject cannot grasp hold of its own bounds or origins, since it would need to get outside itself in order to do so, and this (since we can always ask '*who* is outside herself?') is impossible. God's invisibility is the same kind of invisibility as that of the inner self, not that of some exceptionally high-flying aircraft.

Once the Almighty and all his works had been generally discredited, however, the question of the source of our freedom was bound to reappear. For the modern epoch, it is now not God but humanity which is the eternal author of itself, conjuring itself up out of its own unsearchable depths without visible means of support. The modern conception of freedom as pure self-determination is among other things a secularized version of the Almighty, who has now descended to earth as an anarchist. Yet this, as Friedrich Nietzsche recognized, is hardly much of an advance. Far from having disappeared from history, God has simply been replaced by an alternative supreme entity known as Man. Panic-stricken at the loss of its absolute grounds, humanity has plugged the gap with the nearest thing to hand, namely itself. For Nietzsche, it is business as usual under a new proprietor. It is true that Man has the virtue of actually existing, which had always proved a signal disability in the case of his Creator. As with an indolent office worker, God's absenteeism proved a major drawback to his career prospects. A palpable image of freedom seems preferable to an invisible one; yet since the freedom in question is impalpable of its very essence, it is not clear that a concrete representation of it could be anything but a contradiction.

In Nietzsche's view, the death of God necessarily entails the death of Man. Man is just a stand-in for his celestial manufacturer, an artificial support machine for keeping God alive. To kick away the metaphysical foundations of humanity is inevitably to decentre humanity itself. Humanism is an ideology which disavows the death of God, and Man is a fetish filling the abyss which is himself. Ironically, Nietzsche failed to notice that in this project of decentring God, Christianity had got there before him. In the humanity of Christ, the image of the Father as august metaphysical principle is already dethroned.

Since limits make us what we are, the idea of absolute freedom is bound to be terroristic. This is certainly the case for Hegel, who finds such absolute freedom epitomized in the French Revolution and names it 'the freedom of the void'.[3] Such liberty has a taste of death about it—but a death which is struck empty of meaning, 'the sheer terror of the negative that contains nothing positive, nothing that fills it with a content'.[4] This purely negative brand of liberty, so he considers, is a 'fury of destruction' which can break with the *ancien régime* but proves incapable of building another in its place. This is a logical incapacity, not an empirical one, since whatever such freedom might fashion would inevitably constitute a constraint on it. It can feel alive, Hegel observes, only in the act of destruction—a comment which will prove significant later, when we come to consider the problem of evil. Aspiration is thus strangely close to a kind of nihilism. The act or object which might prove equal to this furious freedom is a kind of void, a fantastic shadow cast by the defectiveness of all actual things. This freedom is a species of absolute refusal, and thus anticipates in its vacancy the absolute negativity of death. It smacks of the negative freedom of the 'metaphysical' terrorist, a type we shall be looking at later, who would consume the whole world in his sublime fury. Only death would truly satisfy such an implacable refusal, rather as the absolute freedom which pursues an infinite war on terror—the 'bad' sublime of our own era—could be satisfied only by turning the world into a wasteland. As long as there are others, there are always potential threats. Freedom can never be complete except in pure solitude.

Having laid waste its surroundings, it is natural in Hegel's view that this brand of freedom should end up consuming itself. Even its own impalpable existence proves to be too much of a barrier. It is so allergic to bounds that it cannot even abide itself, and thus ends up disappearing down the black hole of its own negativity. So it is that the French revolutionaries themselves come to fill the tumbrils. Like a hunger striker, the revolution begins to consume its own body. As Ulysses warns in his great hymn to social order in Shakespeare's *Troilus and Cressida*:

> Then everything includes itself in power,
> Power into will, will into appetite,
> An appetite, an universal wolf,
> So doubly seconded with will and power,
> Must make perforce an universal prey,
> And last eat up himself.   (I. iii)

It is not hard to see the bearing of this self-consuming on our own political world. In the drive to safeguard liberty, the West finds itself increasingly in danger of eradicating it. Preventing terror means stealing its clothes. Freedom is so precious that even despotism is permitted in its name. It is true that there is no point in enjoying civil liberties if you are dead. But it is also worth enquiring whether a life bereft of them is entirely worth living. One does not look forward with any great relish to a situation in which the West has nothing left to protect but its profits. It is true, however, that suppressing your own citizens is a more effective way of combating terrorism than it may appear, since if you convert yourself into a mirror-image of your auto-cratic antagonists, it is questionable why they should wish to destroy you. A certain kind of criminal itches to turn the honest burgher into his own image and likeness, which is no doubt why Fagin is so fascinated by Oliver Twist.

There are those in the West who imagine that Islamic fundamentalists maim or murder as they do because they are envious of Western freedoms. This was always an absurd argument, since fundamentalists envy such freedoms about as much as they long to hang out in Amsterdam cafés smoking dope and reading Simone de Beauvoir. As the West takes to liquidating some of its own liberties, however, it begins to discredit this case by its own actions. When you end up protecting yourself from fundamentalist violence by denying freedom, both parties can be judged to have lost and won.

At its zenith, then, absolute liberty keels over from everything to nothing, an inversion by which Shakespeare's imagination is recurrently gripped. To begin with, absolute freedom seems a positive kind of negation: to be nothing in particular is to harbour the potential to become anything whatsoever.[5] It ends by being negation pure and simple. Shakespeare's Macbeth is an instructive example. Aiming to be all, he overreaches himself, mars his own power, and topples headlong into the realm of pure nothingness signified in the play by the three witches—nameless, bodiless, ambiguous creatures whose negativity gradually infiltrates the kingly protagonist until it dissolves all determinate meaning and identity to a garbled, absurdist, arbitrarily serial narrative, a tale told by an idiot signifying nothing. In the world of Shakespeare it is the Fool, signifier of weakness, finitude, and mortality, who travels in the opposite direction. The Fool is a kind of nothing; but in the act of acknowledging his own hollowness he discovers a determinate kind of identity. To confess one's limits is to transcend them; in fact, we could not identify a limit unless we could already dimly see our way beyond it. Like the figure of the scapegoat, which we shall be encountering later, the Fool plucks something out of nothing. Two negatives make a positive: by doubling his negligibility, raising it to ironic self-consciousness, he comes to transcend it.

To reject absolute freedom is to assent to one's death—a

phenomenon which that freedom finds notably hard to stomach. On the contrary, it is in frantic pursuit of eternal life— meaning not a transfigured version of life as we know it, but an endless supply of the existence we have already. It is the achievement of the middle class to 'horizontalize' heaven, in the doctrine known as progress. Heaven is just an infinite surplus of the same—a traditional description, as it happens, of hell.

In Hegel's eyes, absolute freedom cannot have any determinate content. If it did it would be restricted by it, and so would not be absolute. He speaks of such freedom in the *Phenomenology of Spirit* as 'the sheer terror of the negative that contains nothing positive, nothing that fills it with a content'.[6] If freedom is in the name of specific goals, then it takes its cue from what lies beyond it, and so can no longer be absolute. To step from Hegel to Kant: I am not truly free if I act out of my needs, interests, and desires, since my liberty is then dependent on matters which are external to it. To act as a woman, a peace campaigner, or a Portuguese is to be less than unconstrained. Pure freedom means acting in a way absolved from all specific interests and desires—which is to say, acting in a kind of abyss. 'Absolute' means 'absolved from'. At such times I am no longer hemmed in—but only because there is no longer any substantive selfhood to be curbed. The truly free action is the one which springs from the purest selfhood, which is also where we are most nullified. We can arrive at this Omega point only by subtracting from all that we concretely are, rather as a symbolist poet might dream of unpacking the very heart of meaning by dispensing with the tiresome obfuscations of language.

At its most perfected, then, freedom would appear to vanish altogether. Absolute liberty is entirely vacuous, since having abolished all particularity it leaves us with no reason why we should act in one way rather than another. We are so thrillingly omnipotent that we are left muscle-bound. Visiting a sick relative is a free act, and so is stifling him with his pillow the moment the nurse's back is turned; but freedom of this sort is no guide to which act may be preferable to the other. It is a purely formal concept. In this sense, the freedom which modern civilization prizes as its spiritual essence is also a kind of vacancy at its heart.

Absolute freedom spells the death of difference. In the *Phenomenology*, Hegel links this dissolution of difference with the levelling power of death, and with what he calls 'the *terror* of death'.[7] Absolute freedom is Thanatos in the flesh. A frenziedly abstract drive rides roughshod over concrete particulars—but since it cannot find an image of itself in any of them, it loses grip on itself and lapses into a kind of nothing. Even the difference between the custodians of state power and their insurrectionary opponents begins to fade, not least when you use torture to drive out terror. In a classically paranoid scenario, the West begins to merge, Pentheus-like, into the image and likeness of its antagonists, who were never in any case as alien as they appeared. And this, as we have suggested already, is just what those antagonists have in mind. For you to bring your own liberties into disrepute is far more drastic a discrediting than if your culture were to be denounced from outside. In a judo-like manœuvre, the West risks being brought to the ground by its own unwieldy strength. Liberty itself becomes suffocating, compulsive, unfree. It becomes a prisoner of itself. As Karl Moor cries in Schiller's play *The Robbers*, 'Oh, fool that I was, to suppose that I could make the world a fairer place through terror, and uphold the cause of justice through lawlessness' (Act 5, Scene 2).

In Georg Büchner's drama *Danton's Death*, Danton asks 'How long are we mathematicians of the flesh in our hunt for the ever elusive x to continue to write our equations with the bleeding fragments of human limbs?' In this extraordinary image, the Jacobins or state terrorists are seen as in hot pursuit of some phantasm—call it Justice or Liberty, Truth or Democracy—which in its virulent abstractness is the sworn foe of the flesh. By carving up that carnal stuff, rearranging its bits and pieces into elegant algebraic formulas, they hope to scrawl the equations from which this bodiless abstraction may fall out as a solution. To redeem humankind, they are ready to break into its flesh in order to lay violent hands on the ghostly Idea which secretes itself there. Today, a similar scenario is unfurling in the fantasy-ridden politics of some Western nations, which hope to save peoples less blessed than themselves by first destroying them, then breaking open their corpses to find the word Democracy inscribed on their hearts.

The kind of terrorism which hangs out in the marketplaces of Damascus or the mountains of Montana involves a similar combination of violence and moral idealism. In this sense, it is a monstrous parody of the form of life it opposes. Capitalist society is an extraordinary amalgam of idealism and cynicism, the angelic and the demonic, cloaking its scramble for profits in edifying pieties. Nowhere is this more obvious than in the United States, home of high-minded religious zeal as well as mean-minded material self-interest. As de Tocqueville notes in his *Democracy in America*, 'Religious insanity is common in the United States.' (It is true, however, that Western civilization, not least the British, adheres by and large to what one might call the alcohol counsellor's view of religion: It is all very well as long as it does not begin to interfere with your everyday life. This is also the view which corporate executives tend to adopt of morality.)

Terrorism reflects this unity of the ideal and the cynical. On the other hand, there is its demonic or gleefully nihilistic face: Look, this is what your precious Western civilization amounts to—just a heap of smouldering flesh blown empty of value, just so much raw, unsignifying matter scattered to the winds like so many bleeding limbs. Yet look also at the angelic ideals in whose name we pull your house down around your ears. It is our exalted idealism which inspires us to exterminate you like scum.

In the earlier years of the capitalist system, this split between the angelic and the demonic posed less of a problem. A solution to it, known as Protestantism, lay conveniently to hand. The language of Protestantism was worldly and unworldly at the same time, providing just the connection one needed between the metaphysical and the mundane. Could not the making of profit itself be a sign of spiritual election? Perhaps we had over-estimated the Almighty's disdain for double entry book-keeping. Perhaps nothing delighted his heart more than the sight of a bulging bank account. What sank this pious doctrine almost without trace was not only the discrediting of religion in general, but the shift from industrialism to post-industrialism—from the manufacturing phase of the capitalist system to the epoch of consumption. For it was rather more plausible to believe that God wanted you to be thrifty, prudent, and industrious, to discipline your desires and defer meekly to authority, than that he wanted you to watch hard-core porn, buy a fleet of private aircraft, and consume a monstrous amount of junk food. Consumerism thus helped to snap the link between the material and the metaphysical.

What could be retrieved from the rubble, however, was the idea of freedom. For freedom is a conveniently ambiguous idea, one which couples a high-minded spiritual sense with a less edifying material one. In fact, it is an idiom in which the one can be ceaselessly translated into the other. Freedom signifies a range of precious human rights, as well as a rationale for launch-ing murderous strikes on foreign cities. It is the unquenchable spirit of humanity and the right to shoot unarmed domestic intruders through the back. Small farmers are bankrupted in its name, and hospitals piled high with charred bodies. As an idea suspended between the spirit and the flesh, it is one of the few discourses which can be spoken with equal enthusiasm by arch-bishops and casino owners, oilmen and Oxford philosophers.

Hegel is no admirer of absolute freedom; but he sees it, as he sees most unpalatable things, as playing an essential role in the unfolding of human history. He is not the kind of thinker for whom anything on a grand scale happens by accident. When freedom first emerges in the form of political emancipation, it has a tendency to run wild, giddy with its own exuberant energies. But it will settle down in time to a more sober, constructive sort of existence. One can thus look upon such events as the French Revolution with the mingled tolerance and anxiety of a parent who discovers that his teenage daughter has just emptied the gin bottle. It is alarming, but she will grow out of it. Yet though middle-class society does indeed outgrow its hot-headed adolescence, it never sheds a secret nostalgia for its old dissolute ways, and at times of political crisis it tends to revert to them. In the past few years we have been witnessing one such reversion, as in response to the moral obscenities of terrorism, a headstrong Western absolutism threatens to trample under foot the very checks and constraints which are supposed to help it flourish.

Liberal capitalist orders do not, of course, hold that freedom is in practice absolute. Each individual's liberty must be curbed by the rights of others. My right not to be constrained by others itself involves submitting to constraints. The problem, however, is that the politics of this brand of freedom are at odds with the metaphysics of it. Metaphysically speaking, this freedom has no end or origin. You cannot ask where it comes from, any more than you can enquire where God comes from. Absolute freedom, to be sure, is unlike God in various other senses. It is intensely lonely, for example, whereas there are three of God to keep each other company. But it also differs from God in the sense that God is constrained by himself. He could not be malicious, dim-witted, or grossly incompetent and still be divine. He is not at liberty to be cruel or capricious. Like a hamster, he is incapable of being untrue to his own nature—though with a nature as magnificent as that, this would seem a fairly trifling defect.

Absolute freedom, likewise, cannot not be freedom; but since it has no definitive content, this commits it to nothing. It does, however, resemble the Almighty in other ways. Neither, for example, could logically have had a Creator. And absolute freedom, like God, is a law unto itself, which is the literal meaning of 'autonomy'. If it is dependent on a source or shaped by an end, it ceases to be absolute. Like the process of capital accumulation, it knows no natural closure. As Thomas Hobbes remarks, sovereignty cannot bind itself. If it is to be free to shackle the whole of creation, it must itself be unchained. Seeking to restrain absolute freedom is like trying to rope the wind. If it were finite, it would not be itself.

This kind of liberty, then, must go all the way down. Because it constitutes the very kernel of identity, it is what we are prepared to die or kill for. Since whatever is boundless is a potential source of terror, capitalist orders bear within themselves a residue of the sublime fury which helped to bring them to birth. The negative freedom of revolutionary terror lingers on, much mollified and attenuated, in the negative liberty of orthodox liberal doctrine. This is not to suggest that all businessmen and politicians are budding Dantons. Liberal freedoms represent an incalculably precious heritage—one without which any socialism is unquestionably sunk from the outset. Socialists are not the enemies of liberals, but those who take their creed most seriously. Yet if those liberties are as robust as they are, it is partly because the powers which they seek to restrain are inherently anarchic. When these powers grow insolent and overbearing, they provoke into existence a different kind of anarchy, in an inverted mirror-image of themselves.

Freedom does not in fact go all the way down. What self-determination we can achieve exists within the context of a more fundamental dependency. The free self belongs to a dense, indecipherable history, and the ground or earth from which it was torn loose persists unmasterably within it. In the Oedipus myth, this is symbolized by the king's wounded foot, a primordial injury which maintains a ghostly presence within his very name ('Swollen Foot'). Oedipus receives back his identity from an enigmatic source, which the ancient Greeks know as the gods. Like the rest of us, he is dependent for his autonomy on the Other—which means among other things that he is woven out of the freedoms of others as well as out of his own. If the Other is as opaque as the Delphic oracle, it is among other reasons because these free actions are so intricately intertwined that it is hard to tell where one human agent stops and another begins. 'Who is acting here?' is a valid question in such a condition, or even 'Who is desiring?', as 'Who is in pain here?' is not. In the Oedipus myth, this garbling or scrambling of separate identities is pressed to the point of incest. It is hard to say who you are if you are both son and husband to the same person.

Absolute freedom must in practice buckle down to definitive limits. From its own standpoint, however, these limits are no part of its nature, any more than being handcuffed is part of a burglar's nature. For non-absolutists, by contrast, freedom's limits are internal to it as well as external. One's freedom is shaped from inside by the demands of those through whom alone it can be realized. My freedom must posit the freedom of others, not just respect it—and posit it in a way which makes it constitutive of my own. Only in this way can freedom shed its potentially terroristic character.

Liberty, then, always harbours a certain licence at its heart, which it can neither eradicate nor endorse. There is a lawlessness inherent in the capitalist status quo, given that it appeals to order and authority in the name of a latently anarchic liberty. Absolute freedom is the repressed desire or political unconscious of a decent, reasonable, civic capitalism. It is the fantasy of the capitalist who dreams that he is without competitors, even though he knows that this would spell his own demise along with that of his rivals. Freedom of this kind is a despotic force, which like an autonomous work of art is loyal only to the law of its own being. As a species of permanent transgression, it exists only in the act of bucking the law, shucking off curbs, and kicking over the traces. Because it is purely negative it is without a body, and thus sublimely beyond the reach of representation.

In this sense, the central principle of middle-class civilization cannot be figured within it. This elusive, quicksilver thing called freedom slips through the net of its representations and can be felt only as a cryptic silence or shadowy presence. For Immanuel Kant, we know that we are free because we catch ourselves behaving that way out of the corner of our eye; but we cannot capture this mercurial force in a cognitive theory or a sensuous image. Bourgeois society is thus a breaker of icons, and the very core of middle-class humanity is a sort of nothingness. Like God, this foundation is no more than a void, a pure emptiness which, as emptiness tends to do, goes all the way down. We can feel our freedom from the inside with incomparable immediacy, but we cannot make a graven image of it. As science comes to net more and more truth, philosophy insists that the knower himself, whose essence is freedom, is as inaccessible as the remotest star.

There is, then, something curiously disembodied about the freedom which fuels the established system—a system which for all its obsession with the consumable harbours a virulent hostility to the material. If it hankers after the palpable world, it is among other things because it wants to pound it to pieces in its murderous infantile aggression. In this light, the radical Islamic view that the West is a squalidly materialist place is true in one sense but false in another. Absolute freedom, like desire, rages at the various bits and pieces it stuffs into its infinite maw, all of which threaten to baulk it in the very act of gratifying it. Desire is secretly as monkish as asceticism, ransacking whatever comes to hand only in order to close its fist over infinity. It is an infinity which the very paucity of its objects brings painfully to its mind. It knows exactly what it is—namely, the opposite of whatever it encounters. Freedom cannot flourish without realizing itself in practice; but it is constricted by its own creations, crestfallen by the contrast between their paltriness and its own boundless potential. In a similar way, the realization of desire is a threat to desire itself. Yet in rejecting particular things in the name of everything, it risks landing itself with nothing. If desire rebuffs all suitors, however, it is also because it is rattled by the fear of its own extinction. Like Keats in the presence of the nightingale, it suspects that its fulfilment would mean its demise. This is why it reaps pleasure (like Keats before the Grecian urn) from teasing, deferring, putting itself in suspense. The prohibition of desire is integral to its flourishing. There is that within desire which is inimical to it, just as there is a despot struggling to get out from absolute freedom.

Absolute freedom is thus never far from the melancholy of a Faust, whose achievements turn to ashes in his mouth. It is affronted by the blemished, unfinished nature of matter, and enraptured by the purity of annihilation. Only by teetering perpetually on the brink of attainment can it avoid the dis-enchantments of fulfilment. It is the exquisite perversity by which we gratify our desire by not enjoying the object of it. 'Things won are done; joy's soul lies in the doing' (I. ii), cries Cressida in Shakespeare's play, while Troilus is painfully con-scious of what Hegel might call the 'bad infinity' of desire: 'This is the monstruosity in love, lady, that the will is infinite, and the execution confin'd; that the desire is boundless, and the act a slave to limit' (III. ii)

Because this form of power lacks a body, it is not forced to feel the wanton damage it wreaks. It is like Lear before the storm. It is true that capitalism at its most sublime and semiotic, in which a Caliban-like grossness of goods is magically trans-muted into an Ariel-like fluidity of codes and signs, still needs its material plant and paraphernalia, which is what makes it so sickeningly vulnerable to assault. Whatever has a body can be smashed to smithereens. Nobody has ever clapped eyes on inflation or the interest rate, but banks and chief executives are alarmingly corporeal. Like finance capitalism, political terror-ism is also diffuse, ubiquitous, and largely invisible, bearing something of the relation to a conventional military force that a laptop does to a typewriter. Yet if it deploys avant-garde technologies, it is in order to strew the flesh of men and women on the streets. The more finely intangible an apparatus, the more brutal the carnage. In this combination of technology and the body, the impalpable and the grossly carnal, terrorism is quintessentially postmodern.

Absolute power drains the world of inherent meaning, so that it can offer less resistance to its designs upon it. But a world without meaning is scarcely worth subjugating in the first place. Freedom is condemned to exercise its powers on a reality which it has itself degraded. To this extent, it is more of a Protestant phenomenon than a Catholic one. A certain vein of radical Protestantism empties the world of intrinsic value in order to entrench the power of God. If things have value and significance in themselves, then this must surely place an unacceptable limit on God's authority. For this line of thought, genocide is not bad in itself, nor is generosity good; they are good or bad only because God wills them to be so. If his law is to be absolute, it must also be arbitrary. But then what merit does it have?

René Descartes was among those who thought in this way. If God is not to be restricted by logic, which would surely be beneath his divine dignity, he must have been able to create a world in which $2 + 2 = 5$. Indeed, he may well have fashioned another universe in which the Ten Commandments exist, but with all the 'nots' left out. It is just our bad luck that we got to live in this universe instead. Like a postmodern philosopher, this God is a supreme anti-essentialist: he made things without natures so as to be unobstructed by them. Anti-essentialism and arbitrary power go hand in hand. If divine omnipotence is to be preserved, essences have to go. If things do not have a density of their own, then both God and humanity can knock them around as the fancy takes them. This kind of God, one might say, has an iron whim. And a certain species of humanity is fashioned in his image. For mainstream theology, by contrast, God wills what is inherently good. The world has a shape and thickness of its own which he is obliged to respect. Otherwise, if it were not autonomous in this way, it would not be *his* world. When it comes to absolute power or freedom, voluntarism and nihilism are sides of the same coin. Reality must be purged of its meaning if it is to be tractable stuff in the hands of its manipulators. Postmodernist constructivism is the latest flourish of this age-old fantasy. Yet how can power thrive without resistance? And what is the point of colonizing a world which has been bleached of value? In trafficking with such a world, how are you not simply plucking out of it with one hand what you have smuggled into it with the other? Like the fall guy in Wittgenstein's *Philosophical Investigations*, it is as though one were to pass money from one hand to the other under the impression that one was making a financial transaction.

As in the French Terror, absolute freedom lives only in the act of negation. Though it sulks at the mildest frustration, it needs obstacles and antagonists in order to come alive. There can be no transgression without boundaries to burst through, yet no boundaries in a world which absolute freedom dissolves to so much amorphous sludge. This need for antagonists is clear enough in contemporary politics: if the Soviets have ceased to play the role of Other on the Western stage, then the Muslims might always act as understudies. It would seem that the West needs to keep conjuring a bogeyman into being, a task greatly facilitated by the fact that there is no shortage of people who detest it. In Freudian terms, desire needs perversely to incite its own opposition. In more prosaic terms, this need for adversaries is known as the armaments industry. There are, to be sure, real and deadly foes around in plenty, whose schemes to rip the heads from the innocent must be thwarted. But enemies also constitute precious evidence of the existence of an objective world, thus lending your own projects some ontological credibility. When power lacks resistance it sinks quickly into narcissism and delusion, like a fabulously rich celebrity or a pampered dictator. Absolute power is at risk of destroying the very conditions which give it meaning. It is not its weakness which threatens to topple it, but its strength.

The Marquis de Sade's fantasy of an indestructible victim, one who can therefore be tortured to eternity, is an imaginative response to this dilemma. The trouble with a dead victim is that he can no longer bear witness to your supremacy. Obliterating your opponent is a way of denying your dependence on him, but only at the cost of being thrust into a crisis of identity. This is true of global politics as well. There are evident benefits to be reaped from conquering the whole planet, but among the less obvious is the fact that it may help to solve the problem of how you are to legitimate your power. For what if you have nobody to legitimate yourself to? What if there is nobody left to be persuaded by your increasingly implausible ideological fictions, since they are all in any case safely under your sway? Might absolute power then be the precondition of truth? Would *this* be the much-heralded end of ideology?

In another sense, however, it is dangerous to have no more globe to conquer. A global identity is a contradiction in terms, since it flattens out the very differences on which any identity depends. 'Everything' implodes into its opposite: to crush those differences beneath your heel is to end up knowing nothing, least of all yourself. There are none so ignorant of geography as those with their military bases in every quarter of the planet. It is possible to have satellites which survey every square inch of the globe while producing schoolchildren who think that Malawi is a Disney character. The fate of such cultures is to be marooned eternally with themselves, like some bar-room bore. In Kierkegaard's phrase, they find themselves a 'sovereign without a country'.

Neo-conservative fanaticism is often regarded as an alarming aberration from the civilized Western norm. And so in a way it is. It is grossly embarrassing for liberal capitalist societies, which are used to seeing ideological fanatics as other people, to confront the truth that its own common sense is an ideology as well, and one which can be every bit as extremist as Moonies or Maoists. But aberrations, as we have seen, are also significant for the light they cast on the norm itself. The capitalist order is the only historical culture in which transgression is not only ordained but obligatory—in which everyday life would stumble to a halt without a ceaseless vaulting of boundaries, garbling of distinctions, bending of norms, and flouting of taboos. It comes as no surprise, then, that it was in this form of life that the secret complicity between law and desire was first brought to light, in the shape of psychoanalytic theory. This is a system which can stand still only by maintaining a hectic gallop, and its stability is no more than a constantly renegotiated disorder. Because an individualist order is inherently formless, the powers which mould it into shape have to be foisted arbitrarily on to it, and an imposed order is always the most precarious.

For much of the time, to be sure, the capitalist sublime is held securely in check by what Burke would call the 'beauty' of civil society. Neo-conservatism breaches this settlement by taking the absolute nature of freedom with insolent literalness. If freedom is absolute, how can it not be its own law in practice as well as theory? Why should it need the obstructive apparatus of rights, consensus, diplomacy, legitimation, and the like? If liberty is supremely valuable, how on earth could there be an excess of it? To think in these terms is indeed an aberration— but one which reveals the potentially deviant nature of the norm.

Absolute freedom knows no inner constraint. It can be held in place only by moral, legal, and political forms imposed upon it from the outside, which means that capitalist society betrays a permanent conflict between its form and its content. This is surely one reason why its philosophers have dreamt of a kind of form which would be wholly internal to its content, and have found this political utopia in the work of art. One would not have expected art to be granted such lavish attention in the thought of a society in which it plays less and less of a practical role; yet from Kant to Derrida, modern Western philosophers have turned again and again to the question of aesthetics. The political implications of organic form is one reason for this pre-eminence of aesthetics in a philistine age, though there are, to be sure, a number of others.[8] The form or law of the artefact is not one arbitrarily foisted upon it; rather, it signifies nothing more than the way in which the content of the work spontaneously organizes itself from the inside. This is not a law or order which is abstractable from the work's sensuous particulars; it is simply the profile traced by their mutual articulation. In this sense, the work of art can gather the unruly materials of everyday life into a shapely whole without losing anything of their vitality. If it is a riposte to political absolutism, it is also an argument against anarchy.

Aesthetic humanism, then, sets its face against both vacuous formalism and shapeless libertarianism. It sees the work of art as reconciling energy and order, individual and universal, flux and stillness, freedom and necessity, time and eternity. In doing so, the art-work becomes an allegory of how one might seal the rift in middle-class society between the stasis of its moral and cultural sphere, and the kinesis of its economic and political worlds. Moreover, if the 'law' of the artefact is invisibly incarnate in the subject-matter it shapes, then the art-work is politically speaking an image of hegemony rather than coercion. Metaphysically speaking, it is a working model of that reconciliation of love and law which was once known as God.

Because its form is no more than the inner shape of its content, the art-work has a smack of necessity about it. It can offer an image of freedom which is more than mere contingency. Everything about it seems to happen exactly as it should, so that to describe a certain order of words as 'poetic' is to claim that they could not have come about otherwise without grievous loss. This is by no means the case with the modern world in general, where, as we have seen, the idea of freedom seems inseparable from the scandal that nothing at all needs to exist, least of all ourselves. It is agreeable that there are brandies and brain surgeons, but it is not ineluctable. What we need for our security, it appears, is a kind of freedom which could not not exist; and whereas pre-modern civilization found this in God, modernity is forced to substitute for this august solution the far less popular, far less effectual idea of art.

4

Saints and Suicides

IF freedom is a curse as well as a blessing, it is because it can be used to lay waste as well as to create. This is why, like all sacred powers, it needs to be hedged round with a thick mesh of caveats and prohibitions. What is supremely valuable about it is also what is most dangerous. We might call this power to destroy an abuse of freedom, but it is an abuse which must be permanently possible if freedom is to flourish, and to this extent is part of its nature. An animal which can perform life-saving surgery can also torture. *Felix culpa* means that when it comes to freedom, you have to take the kicks with the ha'pence.

In any case, creation and destruction are not always the alternatives they might appear, as hunger strikers and suicide bombers can testify. Hunger strikers are those who die of their own lethal will. The will becomes a foreign body in their flesh, eating it away. Whatever their actual beliefs they are in this respect children of the Enlightenment, since for the Enlightenment the will is for the most part a force which dominates matter and presses it imperiously into its service. For the hunger striker, the matter in question is his or her own flesh. The final triumph would be the disappearance of matter altogether, as the protestor dwindles to nothing beneath the ferocious force of his own resolution.

Most hunger strikers, however, hope to live, which is not the case with suicide bombers. The point of hunger striking is not just to refuse food but to refuse one's oppressor's food, thus unmasking the irony of being kept alive by those who in some more fundamental sense are out to destroy you. It is not just a question of dying, but of laying one's death dramatically at someone's door. Hunger striking and suicide bombing are alike, however, in that both are self-contradictory actions. If they are symptoms of weakness and despair, they are also theatres of defiance. The suicide bomber proclaims that even death would be preferable to his wretched form of life—indeed, that this way of life *is* a form of death, of which one's actual death is merely the material consummation. The act of self-dispossession writes theatrically large the self-dispossession which is your routine existence. Laying violent hands on oneself is in this sense simply a more graphic image of what the enemy is doing to you any-way, and so converts your powerlessness into a public spectacle. Death is a solution to your existence, but also a commentary on it.

Yet such a death is also discontinuous with one's existence, as well as of a piece with it. By disposing freely of his life, the suicide bomber hopes to draw attention to the contrast between this extreme form of self-determination, and the absence of such autonomy in his everyday life. If only he could live as he dies, he would not need to die. Destroying yourself is a sign of just how dramatic a transformation would be needed to make your daily life tolerable. But it is also a desperate alternative to that change. Like the tragic protagonist, the suicide bomber transcends his destiny by freely submitting to it, thus becoming victor and victim together. Suicide bombing is the last word in passive aggression. It is vengeance and humiliation in a single gesture. By actively consenting to be nothing, the suicide aims to become something of great price. Like a number of tragic protagonists, too, the bomber is not notable for his fastidious-ness about how many innocent lives he takes with him. By turning himself into an object, rather than enduring such shame at the hands of others, he becomes for a fleeting moment a free subject—a condition which, as we shall see later, is that of the scapegoat too, though the scapegoat is innocent and the suicide bomber is not. At least his death is now *his* death, rather than part of the mass production of death which goes on around him.

If modernity is about having a room of one's own, it is also about having a death of one's own—an event which, so Rilke claims in *The Notebooks of Malte Laurids Brigge*, is growing increasingly rare. Nietzsche remarks that there is nothing more banal than death, perhaps with the implication that a spiritual aristocrat like himself should not submit without protest to the vulgarity of meeting a fate he shares with plebeians. The suicide bomber's violence is among other things a gesture of defiance of this mass-produced world, one in which he himself figures as no more than a cypher. In a social order which seems progressively more depthless, transparent, rationalized, and instantly communicable, the brutal slaughter of the innocent reinstates the opaque, the excessive, the irreducibly particular. Terrorism is an assault on meaning as well as on materiality, a Dadaist or Surrealist 'happening' pressed to an unthinkable extreme. It is spectacle as well as slaughter.

In Conrad's novel *The Secret Agent*, Mr Vladimir spurs Verloc on to a terrorist act which would be not only fearful but absurd. 'A bomb outrage to have any influence on public opinion now,' he tells him, 'must go beyond the intention of vengeance or terrorism. It must be purely destructive. It must be that, and only that, beyond the faintest suspicion of any other object . . . what is one to say to an act of destructive ferocity so absurd as to be incomprehensible, inexplicable, almost unthinkable; in fact, mad? Madness alone is truly terrifying . . . I would never dream of directing you to organize a mere butchery . . .' (ch. 2). So Vladimir suggests blowing up not a theatre or restaurant, but Greenwich Observatory. To do this, he believes, would make the point that terrorism is more symbolic or expressive than instrumental. Yet he also speaks scornfully of the Observatory as the symbol of the middle class's fetishistic faith in science, thus partly undercutting his own point. If you want your act of terror to be truly absurdist, why not blow up a public lavatory? Vladimir thus makes the point against his own intentions that political terror is not in fact sheerly purposeless. This does not necessarily make it any the less objectionable, but it certainly makes it less lunatic. In any case, planning an outbreak of madness is reliable evidence of your sanity. It is as self-disproving as throwing a stranger off a train in order to prove that there can be a purely motiveless deed.

Even so, one can still see some forms of suicide bombing as a murderous version of the artistic avant-garde, a Dadaist conjuring of the chaotic, ineffable, and unintelligible from the anaemic certainties of the everyday world. Like the avant-garde, suicide bombing aims to explode the social game itself, rather than simply to make a new move within it. It is meant to ravish the mind as well as fracture the flesh, warping the space of the intelligible until it implodes. It is the ultimate act of defamiliarization, transforming the everyday into the monstrously unrecognizable. It is meant to cut the ground metaphorically as well as literally from beneath our feet. Shock and outrage are part of its meaning, not mere side-effects.

Those excluded from the public sphere thus act out a public drama of their own creation. It is just that those who play the bystanders never get to choose their parts. The suicide bomber triumphs over his or her adversaries since he or she is prepared to perish while they are not. The final freedom is not to fear death—a fear which keeps us compliantly in our places. It is thus that the sluggish Barnadine in *Measure for Measure* unwittingly gets the better of his superiors. Barnadine must be persuaded to die willingly—not because he is unwilling, but because he does not care one way or the other, an indifference or ataraxy which the ruling order finds far more disquieting. It is death, or the dread of it, which is the support of civility, as for Burke the sublime is the infrastructure of the beautiful. Those who have nothing to lose are deeply dangerous, which is why the power which has brought them to this point has failed. Staring death in the eye is the most foolproof way of ensuring that such power has no hold over you. By dying to yourself, as Barnadine does, you pre-empt death's authority. To live with death quarantines you from failure, swaddles you against harm, and insulates you from anxiety. It is really quite a life.

To blow yourself up is not necessarily to be morbidly in love with your own mortality. Hunger strikers and suicide bombers hold that life is precious, otherwise they would not be doing what they do. The hunger striker wants her demands met so that she can eat again. It is just that both parties consider that what lends your life fundamental value is whatever you are prepared to give it up for. If nothing is meaningful enough to die for, what is the point of living? The act of abandoning your life then allows this Cause to shine out as the luminous backdrop to your own extinction. In dying, you force a contrast between your own mortality and the imperishability of what you die for. It is the same as in the sublime, which makes us feel its immensity by contrast with our own negligibility. The more you are diminished, the more it is enhanced. Yet there is a sleight-of-hand involved here, too. You do not die after all, since this incorruptible Cause is the kernel of your own existence, the form in which you will live forever.

In this sense, political suicide is a grotesque parody of what for Immanuel Kant is the purely ethical act—one motivated by a supreme disinterestedness which sets aside personal interests in the name of a higher duty. In this pure act, so the theory goes, the self is transformed and reborn—or at least it would be in the case of the suicide bomber, were it not that he has just placed himself beyond the reach of rebirth in the most definitive of ways. But you can always see this transformation as displaced onto his or her community, who through his action will be regenerated. In reality, however, such Kantian acts, absolved of all 'pathological' elements, are egregiously hard to come by, and suicide bombing is no exception. You die in hatred and despair as well as in faith and hope. And there is always the beguiling thought of paradise to ease your passage. The genuine martyr is the one who lets everything go, even the hope of salvation. The suicide bomber, by contrast, usually has one eye fixed firmly on his eternal reward, just as the bogus sort of martyr is merely trying to inveigle his way into the club of paradise by charming the proprietor. He has not, after all, escaped the logic of exchange value. The well-nigh impossible paradox of true martyrdom, as Thomas recognizes in T. S. Eliot's *Murder in the Cathedral*, is that only by not contemplating the fruits of your action can it prove fruitful. Otherwise you are simply engaged in a rather sordid trade-off. This kind of action troubles the distinction between 'rational' and 'non-rational' behaviour: you must not calculate the outcome, but not because you are engaged in some exotic *acte gratuit*. And this is not a paradox confined to such exceptional events, as those who fail to impress others because they are trying to impress them can no doubt testify.

Some centuries ago, what Western men and women were prepared to die for in great numbers was religion. This is still true of various other regions of the globe, which is one reason why the West has something of a political problem on its hands. In modern times, however, as Benedict Anderson points out in his *Imagined Communities*, what people are ready to perish for is the nation. Nationalism is a lingering trace of transcendence in a secular world. Like God, the nation is immortal, indivisible, invisible yet all-encompassing, without origin or end, worthy of our dearest love, and the very ground of our being. Like God, too, its existence is a matter of collective faith. There would not be a nation unless we believed that there was. It does not exist in the sense that the Great Barrier Reef does. If the nation survives by faith, it equally involves political hope, not least for its future liberation; and it is also a domain of charity or fraternal affection. 'Filling out the empty place of the Supreme Good,' comments Slavoj Žižek, 'defines the modern notion of Nation.'[1]

Hunger strikers are out to transform weakness into power. They can exercise their victory over the forces which hold them down by cheating them of the only part of themselves which they can control: their bodies. By depriving their masters of this manipulable part of themselves, they become invulnerable. Nothing is less masterable than nothing. Their conquest over self is so complete that there is nobody left to claim the spoils. Victory and defeat are thus indistinguishable. Yet killing yourself may also be a way of keeping death's terrors at arm's length. What looks like a resolute confrontation of your morality can also be an evasion of it. What if the very act of extinguishing the ego were simply the final flamboyant assertion of it? Self-dispossession may be the ultimate form of self-proprietorship. He who kills himself, writes Maurice Blanchot in *The Literary Space*, is a great affirmer of the present, since he wants this moment of self-extinction to be an absolute one which will neither pass nor be surpassed. In Blanchot's view, voluntary death is a self-undoing act, affirming the supremacy of the will in the very act of giving it up as a bad job. Since death is what unhinges all our projects and remains a foreigner to our decisions, there is something inescapably self-cancelling about forging a project out of it. The philosopher Emmanuel Levinas comments in his *Time and the Other* that death marks the end of all heroism and virility; but the truth is that it can be a version of them as well.

The suicide, Blanchot argues, demonstrates a kind of strength suitable only for a citizen of the world. It is the sort of resolution which belongs squarely to the sphere it takes you out of. Your death becomes your worldly possession, to be disposed of as a kind of property. Destroying yourself involves a curious kind of life-in-death, since it implies that one can dispose of one's own nothingness in sovereign fashion, and this at the very instant when one proclaims the futility of action and the emptiness of power. In Blanchot's eyes, the suicide may be a tragic figure, but he or she is also, inescapably, an ironist.

Power may drive the hunger striker to her death; but in doing so it deprives itself of anyone to subjugate, which is what the hunger striker is banking on. She will force authority to betray its own vacuity, slipping through its fingers and leaving it grasping at thin air. If power overreaches itself, it ends up crushing the life out of what it had hoped to control, leaving itself with no one to lord it over and thus chalking up a pyrrhic victory. Absolute power is a kind of living death: it needs to turn things into corpses of themselves if it is to secure its hold over them. In this sense, the hunger striker is an inverted image of that power, since he vanquishes his adversary by putting paid to himself. In affirming his absolute sovereignty over himself, he wipes himself out of existence. The price he pays for his supremacy is non-being.

To die at a time of your own choosing is to dispose of your life in the manner of an absolute monarch. Yet if you are your own master, it follows that you are also your own slave. The consequence of this act of freedom is the end of freedom. Just as the act of sacrifice brings together an all-powerful priest and a powerless victim, so the suicide bomber, who presides ritually over his own dismemberment, is both together. As a sacrificial scapegoat, he hopes to pass by this ritual self-immolation from weakness to power. What this means in practice, however, is that the only power he has left is the capacity to take charge of his own victimization.

In destroying their own flesh and blood, hunger strikers and suicide bombers bear witness to a power which is in their view even more formidable than the state. The flesh may be corruptible, but in the very process of its dissolution the Idea which spurs them on stands forth radiant, sublime, unkillable. What cannot be annihilated is the very will which drives them to annihilate themselves. To be able to will yourself out of existence is to be godlike indeed. It is both to imitate God and to oust him, since as a creator in your own right you have now usurped his divine prerogative. Suicide is the death of God. He who is ready to kill himself becomes a god, declares Krillov in Dostoevsky's *The Devils*. What more breathtaking form of omnipotence than to do away with yourself for all eternity? Such an act has a smack of immortality about it—ironically, to be sure, since its result is exactly the opposite. Perhaps this is what Jacques Lacan had in mind when he observed that 'suicide is the only successful act'.[2] It is certainly the only *perfect* act, as we shall see later in the case of Conrad's *The Secret Agent*, since there are no loose ends and messy consequences, at least for the agent. Those left behind are not so lucky.

Very few of those branded as terrorists are in fact suicide bombers, and a great many of those who are not are fighting for aims which in other political circumstances their enemies might well regard as legitimate. They themselves, after all, threw off the imperial yoke in their time, and have lent their support to numerous acts of bloody insurrection around the globe. The ideology of suicide bombing is a more rarefied, specialized affair than guerrilla war as such. And even within suicide bombing itself, there is what one might call a pragmatic and a metaphysical strain. As a Satanic version of God, the metaphysically minded suicide bomber, like the mad professor of *The Secret Agent*, hopes to create out of nothing. His radical innovation consists of bringing chaos into being, thus putting Creation into reverse. By blowing a black hole in what God has fashioned, he tries to catapult himself on to equal terms with him. Saints and sinners have more in common with each other than they have with the moral middle classes. Devils are just fallen versions of angels. Nothing is more original and unique than destruction, since you cannot demolish the same bridge twice. You can make an absolute difference to reality not by adding to or reshaping it, but by obliterating it. Yet destruction for the more pragmatically minded suicide bomber is not simply for its own sake. Out of the abyss you scoop in the lives of the guiltless, new life for your own people may spring.

If killing yourself is the only weapon you have to hand—if you have nothing to dispose of but your biology—then you must be poor indeed. But the act is also a savage send-up of your enemy's top-heavy military hardware, to which ten stone or so of flesh and blood may prove more than equal. The insurrectionist who fires off missiles from a donkey cart is a satirist as well as a soldier. In an ominously carnivalesque image, he reverses the clichéd image of the powerless little man crushed by a faceless system.

The death of the suicide bomber is likely to prove far more significant an event than anything in his life. It becomes, in fact, the only truly historic occurrence in the careers of the dumped and disregarded, the point where—having torn small children to shreds and vaporized the blameless—they can feel most intensely alive. Nothing in their life becomes them like the leaving of it. Dying ceases to be useless expenditure. However wretched or depleted, most men and women have one formidable power at their disposal, namely the capacity to die as devastatingly as possible. As the heroine of *Romeo and Juliet* declares: 'If all else fail, myself have power to die.' Death bestows on you a perfection which can only be the envy of the living.

It helps, in surrendering your body, to be assured that it is no immortal part of you. Since the flesh is what is most obviously finite about us, shucking it off must surely be the speediest way to eternity. And if the flesh seems trifling in contrast with the splendours of the soul, robbing others of their bodies appears less of a crime. This is not, in fact, the orthodox teaching of Islam, for which the body is sacred. Nor is this cavalier attitude towards the flesh the doctrine of Christianity, for which redemption is a matter not of the immortality of the soul, but of the resurrection of the body. Alain Badiou is one of the few non-Christian philosophers to have grasped the point that the Pauline distinction between 'flesh' and 'spirit' is not one between body and soul. It is a contrast between two forms of life—the former a question of violence and appetite, the latter a matter of justice and compassion.[3] The one falls under the law, while the other is grounded in love.

Martyrs are not hostile to the body: they give up what they see as precious, not worthless, otherwise their action would lack any sort of merit. Nor do they want to die. They would prefer to live, but given the circumstances fail to see how they can. They do not seek death directly, even if death is an inevitable result of their actions. The same is true of those who leapt from the World Trade Center in 2001 to escape being incinerated. They were not seeking death, even though there was no way they could have avoided it. Nor are martyrs' deaths designed to deprive others of their lives. They make a statement out of their dying, but not a weapon.

Even so, martyrs have their affinities with suicide bombers as well as their differences. Both parties die in the name of life for others, not as an end in itself. The Islamic radical or US anti-government insurgent believes that his death will help to emancipate his people, while the Christian martyr dies rather than betray a faith he regards as vital to human fulfilment. The word 'martyr' means 'witness', and the martyr bears witness to his faith by choosing it over life. But since in his view that faith concerns an abundance of life all round, his action is the reverse of necrophiliac. If it is unreasonable in the short term, it is reasonable in the long term. It sacrifices a short-term benefit for himself to the long-term good of others. Because the martyr will not compromise his principles, being a member of this select category means refusing to sell out, keeping the faith even when it seems futile or inconvenient to do so. The opposite of the martyr is the fair-weather believer. The act signifies a hope for the future, bearing witness to a truth and justice beyond the present. By turning his body into a sign of the absence of these things, the martyr reminds us that the world is not yet fit for them, and thus helps to keep them alive. But whereas the martyr is prepared to stake his life on this, the suicide bomber is prepared to stake *your* life on it. Martyrs such as Rosa Luxemburg or Martin Luther King die so that others may live; suicide bombers die so that others may die so that others may live.

Suicide bombing is a supreme exercise of will, which is part of what binds it to the civilization it opposes. Few faculties are more vital to that form of life than the supreme faculty of free choice. To see the will as a kind of autonomous force—as 'will-power'—is a characteristically modern way of thinking about it, one foreign to the thought of a medieval philosopher such as Thomas Aquinas. Aquinas thought of free will not in this abstract way, but as somehow built into our flesh and blood. Questions of choice, he considered, depended in the end on the make-up of our material bodies. Aquinas is quite materialist about these matters: he believes, for example, that emotion is chiefly a physical affair, and that individuals are thoroughly corporeal creatures. Human beings in his view are bodies of a certain kind, not bodies plus distinct entities called souls. The greatest of all Christian theologians would not have believed that John Lennon's disembodied soul was John Lennon.

For Aquinas, we do not have complete freedom of choice because a certain kind of choosing is implicit in what it means to have (or to be) a human body. And this is not something we can opt for. Human beings in his view have a built-in tendency to the good, or at least to what they conceive of as good. We have an appetite for goodness which is not itself optional, any more than our appetite for nourishment is. The will is not all-powerful, but is constrained by our fleshliness. It is the way our bodies are biased and ballasted towards what strikes us as desirable. We are not neutral with respect to the good. If we were, we would never have any grounds for choosing it. In a similar way, we are not neutral with regard to truth. On the contrary, we are the kind of animal who needs it, just as we need sleep and shelter. For this style of thought, our being is weighted towards truth, even if we continually botch the job of dredging it to light. Original sin means that we are built for truth and happiness but have no spontaneous access to what they mean or how to attain them. St Augustine, the first thinker to use the word 'heart' to denote the seat of the emotions, has also been claimed as the first modern thinker in his belief that we are fundamentally inscrutable to ourselves. Having a heart does not permit of simply looking into it.

Choice, then, does not go all the way down, whatever the liberals and supermarket executives may consider. If freedom were completely unconstrained, then this would mean that it was unconstrained by reasons as well; but without reasons we would have no way of knowing what to choose in the first place. We would not really be capable of acting at all, and our freedom would thus be purely notional. An absolute will is bound to be an arbitrary one, since it refuses to acknowledge anything as inconveniently obstructive as a rational motive. Absolute freedom gives birth to a paralysis of the will. Once more, 'everything' keels over into 'nothing'. Even our freedom is given, at least in the sense that we never signed on for it. We are condemned to be free, but not in the sense that we might be condemned to the gallows. Not everything we do not get to choose is objectionable. This is one of several reasons why Aquinas is not a liberal.

Aquinas sees this built-in appetite for what is desirable as a kind of love. For him as for St Augustine, love comes before both freedom and reason, and is more fundamental than either of them. The will is a kind of primary orientation of our existence. For Augustine, it is the desire which prompts us to uncover the intelligibility of things, opening up truth and understanding. We have a loving inclination towards fulfilment, a natural bent towards well-being. We can choose one end over another, but since our well-being is the end of ends, it cannot figure merely as one option among many. We have an interest in our own flourishing, though not in the sense that we might have an interest in buying up shares in Shell. It will not get us anywhere. We may, to be sure, reason falsely about what counts as flourishing, but we cannot reason ourselves out of our built-in love for it.

On this view, we cannot will what we find undesirable. Even those who choose evil do so because they see it as a good idea. Which is not to say that they stop seeing it as evil. People who commit genocide do so because they see it as a good idea, which does not necessarily mean that they see it as a virtuous idea. Even those rare types whom we shall be considering later, who seem to inflict misery upon others purely for the sake of it, do so because evil for its own sake strikes them as desirable as art for its own sake seemed to Oscar Wilde. This, in fact, may constitute one of the tortures of the damned. If even their malevolence is in the name of some kind of good, then they can never escape being dependent on what they despise. The devil finds himself speaking the language of value *malgré lui-même*, and so can never get out from under God's shadow. He needs goodness to exist so that he can spit in its face.

Satan can thus never live down the social embarrassment of having once been an angel. Like a public-schoolboy turned rock star, his well-heeled past is always liable to catch up with him. Negation cannot help acknowledging the existence of what it seeks to annul. Like Shakespeare's Iago, it pays an unwitting compliment to whatever it is intent on tearing to pieces. It cannot avoid conceding a certain priority to it, rather as truth must logically take priority over lying. To cry with Milton's Satan 'Evil, be thou my good!' is to recognize the force of virtue in the act of spurning it. The cynic sails as close as possible to evading this dilemma, since he denies not just this or that value, but value as such. Yet this must seem to him a worthwhile thing to do. To transgress in style, you would need to transgress transgression itself. And this is beyond even the most diabolical of powers.

There is another dilemma here as well. Aquinas thought that there could not be a purely evil being, because being itself was in his view a form of goodness. A thing, he argues, has as much good as it has being—so that to say of God that he is good is not to claim that he is remarkably well-behaved, but that he is overflowing with ecstatic high spirits, enraptured by the inexhaustible fullness of his own being, pulsating with *joie de vivre*. This then creates a problem for the evil, whose very existence puts their own malevolence into question. True evil would have to involve not existing. And this is one meaning of the doctrine of hell, which is about annihilation, not perpetual torment.

Aquinas, then, would have little sympathy with the modern conception of the will as an abstract force bending the world to our desires. This is the will as imperial arrogance and military machine. Those directing such enterprises today are for the most part of puritan stock, for whom life consists of a strenuous series of isolated acts of will. Moral existence is a macho affair. For this square-jawed way of seeing, life is a set of hurdles or challenges. 'Challenge' is Americanese for an utterly irreparable disaster, in a land for which failure is illicit. For Aquinas as for Aristotle, what undercuts this whole virile ideology is the idea of goodness as a habit or disposition, which is what is meant by virtue. One would rather entrust one's life to someone who was spontaneously disposed to reliability than to someone who wrestled anguishedly with his conscience every time the question came up. Virtuous people do not require 'acts of will' in order to be virtuous, which is not to say that they act mindlessly either.

Puritans think of the moral life primarily in terms of duty; and since duty is generally unpleasant, it comes as no surprise that they spend so much of their time in moral torment. Yet the patrician ethic that goodness comes as easily as one's taste in claret, or the sentimentalist version of it as the natural impulse of the heart, are just the flipside of this punitive ethics. The truth is that virtue does indeed involve a degree of sweat, since, as we have seen, it is the kind of thing you have to get good at. Once you have done so, however, you can forget about all those excruciating hours in the moral gymnasium and simply exercise it as a pleasurable capacity in itself.

The omnipotent will which bullies Nature to do its bidding is another name for absolute freedom. When middle-class society is still fresh and buoyant, elated by its victory over its enemies and flushed with unflagging energy, its belief in this will is unbounded. Nothing appears beyond is sublime powers. This ideology is alive and well today in the American dream, for which nothing is impossible once you put your mind to it. A sign on a religious bookstore in New York reads 'What mind can conceive, Man can achieve,' as though the fact that one can easily imagine taking a bite out of Africa is only one step away from actually doing it. Failure, for this crassly hubristic doctrine, is simply lack of will-power. Its pitiless idealism dehumanizes the very humanity it acclaims. There are citizens of the United States for whom the word 'can't' is as pernicious as the word 'communist'. It is a nation in the grip of a frenzied voluntarism, for which limits are always horizons, and for which the frailty and finitude of men and women is a shameful scandal. Former US president Ronald Reagan was much praised for making his compatriots feel good about themselves. This was merely one of his lesser crimes.

Pessimism in such conditions is tantamount to treason. There are no tragic catastrophes, only lessons to be learnt. To be utterly clueless is to be 'on a steep learning curve'. A nation which rejects the notion of tragedy is nowadays starkly confronted with it. The fact that the United States is one of the last nations on earth to understand why it is currently under attack is closely related to the fact that it is. Operation Infinite Freedom has been tried once already, and is known as the Faust legend. In the terrorist attack, those who believe that they are boundless are violently confronted with their own vulnerability. 'They told me I was everything', cries Lear, ' 'tis a lie—I am not ague-proof.' Such fantasists of omnipotence are brought face to face with the finitude of flesh and blood in the most unbearable way imaginable: by being deprived of the stuff. Like the sublime, the terrorist deflates and diminishes us at the very peak of our mastery.

The aim of socialism, by contrast, is not to destroy the flesh but to recall us to our creatureliness. It is this, rather than alternative ways of summoning us to the stars, which is at the nub of its quarrel with the status quo. In fact, it is not out of the question that some of those who only yesterday were celebrating the death of socialism may come in due course to feel positively nostalgic about it, not least those whose offices are rather a long way off the ground. Socialists may wish to see the back of capitalism, but they have no plans to do so with dirty nuclear bombs. Their weapons are trade unions, not typhoid. They are out to expropriate the propertied classes, not exterminate them. Despite the much-vaunted demise of the proletariat, the wretched of the earth have not vanished, merely changed address. They are now to be found in the slums of Rabat rather than the cotton mills of Rochdale; and this is by no means welcome news for the custodians of the status quo, however callowly they may congratulate themselves on having put socialism permanently to rest.

Perhaps, then, those who boast that Marx's proletariat has been sunk without trace should be reaching for the radiation tablets rather than the champagne. For socialists have always rejected the tactics of terror, even if some on the political left have been rather too coy of late in condemning squalid Islamic theocracies. It is the lack of organized political resistance to the present system, of the kind to which socialists have traditionally been dedicated, which encourages it to trample upon the weak, thus stimulating the growth of terror. To this extent, socialism is an antidote to terror, not a variety of it.

Those who complacently proclaim the End of History, or at least were in the habit of doing so until the demolition of the World Trade Center, mean to announce the permanent triumph of capitalism; but it is exactly this crass triumphalism which has stirred the revolt of the masses in the Muslim world, thus launching a whole new historical epoch. The closing down of history has only succeeded in opening it up again. (The same was true, intellectually speaking, of Hegel's celebrated consummation of History, which simply succeeded in generating a whole philosophical lineage—Kierkegaard, Marx, Nietzsche, Adorno, and so on—by way of counter-argument.) And the revolt of the masses, if it furnishes itself with the appropriate weapons, might in one's gloomiest imaginings signal the end of history in a rather less comfortably metaphorical sense of the phrase.

In most nations other than the Panglossian United States, fantasies of omnipotence are fairly short-lived. Once middle-class civilization begins to run into resistance and contradiction, as it does over the course of the nineteenth and twentieth centuries, its sprightliness begins to sour. The idea of the will begins accordingly to modulate into the notion of desire. Desire is the will seen in the light of sober disenchantment. It is the will hollowed out from the inside, infiltrated by some deadly glitch or virus, traced through by a kind of inner flaw which causes our freely chosen actions to stall, boomerang, miss the mark. For the ancient Greeks, this was a tragic flaw, a kind of built-in botching to which they gave the name *hamartia*. It is not, then, that this vision of desire as a sickness of the will or a pathology of freedom emerged only with late modernity. In fact, it is notoriously hard to find a novel idea of any sort. The drama of Jean Racine, for example, sees desire as a frightful calamity, a virulent infection with which we are afflicted as though with cholera or typhoid. But it is in late modernity, not fortuitously, that a full-blown science of desire, known as psychoanalysis, first appears.

Freud learned much in this respect from Arthur Schopenhauer, probably the gloomiest philosopher who ever lived. In Schopenhauer's relentlessly cheerless writings, we catch a more classical concept of the will in the act of shifting over into the notion of desire, as some sublime vacancy, whose intentions are not in the least friendly, comes to insinuate itself at the core of the self. 'All willing,' Schopenhauer comments, 'springs from lack, from deficiency, and thus from suffering.'[4] The malevolent Will installs itself within us as a perpetual hungering and hankering, like a parasite in search of a host body to lodge itself in; yet it is as blankly indifferent to our well-being as the force which stirs the waves. This repulsive, anonymous thing at the core of the self, which we can feel from the inside with all the incomparable immediacy of the smell of a rose or the taste of a pineapple, is implacably alien to us and simply uses us for its own unfathomable ends. We bear an intolerable weight of meaninglessness around with us at the very pith of our selfhood, as though we were permanently pregnant with monsters. Schopenhauer is certainly one source of science fiction.

Like Freudian desire, this useless passion has no grandiose goal, no stately teleology, and is secretly in love only with itself. It lives only in its lack, and its own infinite motion, like Faust, is the nearest it ever approaches to the eternal fulfilment it craves. It is a kind of bad infinity, a sublimity gone awry, an unstaunchable wound cut deep in our being which refuses to heal. We cannot be rid of it, since willing not to will is beyond our power. Like language, desire is a medium into which we fell at birth, and from which there appears no hope of rescue. Any history which might redeem us from it would simply be one of its diseased products. The problem is that we cannot want something without also just wanting pure and simple. But this is no good reason why we should stop wanting altogether. As Kierkegaard reflects in *The Sickness unto Death*, it is great to give up one's desire, but greater still to stick to it after having given it up. It is wise to acknowledge that desire breeds sickness and fantasy, but wiser to recognize that it is, for all that, what makes us what we are.

One of the finest modern anatomies of the death-dealing will is D. H. Lawrence's *Women in Love*, a novel which recognizes with extraordinary acuity that voluntarism and nihilism are sides of the same coin. Gerald Crich, the mine-owner of the story, embodies what the narrator calls 'the plausible ethics of productivity', as a harsh employer and hard-nosed neo-capitalist modernizer. Yet this familiar kind of brute male supremacy is not what makes him so intriguing. Where the novel is most astute is in its perception that Crich's steel-hard will is indissociable from a kind of decadence. Because this will is a form of living death, reaping life from dominion and destruction, Gerald is an image of the living dead, a grisly parody of a genuine person. The more imperiously he wields his power, the more he falls apart on the inside. As his ego hardens, his sensuous life disintegrates, until he is reduced to a hard, shiny carapace concealing a rank mess of emotions. Only the mechanical straining of his will prevents him from collapsing into the void of himself.

It is not surprising, then, that despite being an austerely self-disciplined industrialist, Gerald hangs out with a set of fashionable upper-class hedonists, raffish bohemians who would have trouble in distinguishing a lump of coal from a cauliflower. Since their hunt for outré sensations is a purely cerebral affair, it consorts well enough with the lethal abstractedness of the will. Hermione Roddice's wilful cultivation of the exotic is a case in point. To treat others' bodies as instruments of one's profit or pleasure, and to wallow in the senses for their own sake, come to much the same thing, since neither practice regards sensuous life as significant in itself. The abstract will has come unstuck from the body, treats it merely as a tool, and thus can no longer shape it into significance from the inside. Like this all-devouring will, hedonism is really a form of nihilism, revelling in the very pointlessness of bodily existence. It is when that sensuous life is no longer grasped as purposive that it can be objectified as a fetish to be worshipped, or a commodity to be consumed. For all its excited pursuit of novelty, hedonism is a covert kind of cynicism. Power as an end in itself, and sensation as an end in itself, belong together, as *Women in Love* recognizes. The former is pure form, and the latter pure content. The self-delighting will, which is secretly in love with itself, finds an inverted echo in the erotic gratifications or 'corrupt gorgeousness' of so-called decadence.

Gerald gleans a frisson of gratification from the sheer inhuman mechanism of his mines. What he relishes is the impersonal order they represent, 'strict, terrible, inhuman, but satisfying in its very destructiveness' (ch. 17). He is thus a kind of avant-garde artist, rejoicing in the sterile, anti-humanist flatness of his artefact. In a spasm of *nostalgie de la boue*, his lover Gudrun Brangwen derives a similar 'voluptuous' thrill from the mechanical anonymity of the coal pits. This delight in the mechanically impersonal is a symptom of Thanatos, with its obscene enjoyment of the disfiguring and dehumanizing. It is no accident that we are hovering here, historically speaking, on the very brink of fascism. Fascism is a creed which mingles the cult of the triumphant will with a pornographic fascination with bodies—bodies that seem to it no more than meaningless garbage. Like the Crich coterie in *Women in Love*, it is both entranced by order and gleefully enraptured by chaos. The German artist Loerke, who becomes Gudrun's lover after Gerald, is cynic, sensationalist, and machine-worshipper all in one. Just to ensure that we view him in an appropriately negative light, Lawrence makes him a Jew and a homosexual to boot.

Women in Love, perhaps the most philosophically avant-garde fiction of English modernism, is a post-humanist novel, for which liberal, Christian, humanistic civilization is on the brink of an apocalyptic break-up. In his Nietzschean contempt for pity and paternalism, his cult of impersonality, scorn of compassion, and option for power over love, Gerald marks the end of Man. The novel does not dissent from this post-humanist vision; it simply sees Gerald as representing the wrong version of it. The right version of it is to be found in his friend Rupert Birkin—though Birkin, who is just as disdainful of love, ethical humanism, and social responsibility as Gerald himself, would seem at first glance more his ally than his antagonist. If Gerald is too emotionally anaesthetized to cope with sexual love, Birkin consciously rejects it, seeking with his lover Ursula Brangwen a relationship beyond all relationships. His hunger for the impersonal and pathological aversion to feeling are close to Gerald's own. It is significant that we do not feel inclined to use his first name.

Gerald's existence is a kind of living death, and with a symbolic flourish he meets his end by freezing to death in the snow. For his part, Birkin can contemplate no finer end in life than death itself, the ultimate form of impersonality. Gerald is a spiritual aristocrat who despises the common people, while Birkin reflects that it would be a notable step in human progress if most people were simply to be wiped out. The post-humanism of both characters, in short, is rather more than idly theoretical. Human beings for Birkin are a foulness and defilement, and the novel concedes that his antipathy to them amounts to a kind of illness.

For sheer unpleasantness, then, there seems little to choose between the two. Yet the astonishing audacity of the work lies exactly in this kinship, as it recognizes just how nauseatingly close to Gerald's inner vacuity Birkin's more creative form of negativity actually is. In one sense, Birkin is as much in love with death as Gerald. This is a fiction of Thanatos, in which both male protagonists have a pronounced necrophiliac streak. The difference, however, is that Gerald's life is already a kind of death, whereas Birkin sees death as a necessary prelude to a regenerated existence. He, too, is entranced by the dissolution of the senses and the steady disintegration of the human world. For him, however, all this is not an end in itself, but an essential passage to personal and social rebirth. Death is a dead-end for Gerald but a threshold for Birkin. What the latter seeks is not so much the inhuman as the meta-human: a future beyond the living death of the present which for the time being must remain sublimely unrepresentable. To give this order a name would be to bind it to the corrupted present and so to annul its absolute novelty. Even to fight the old form of life, Ursula argues, is to be complicit with it. You cannot actively construct a new order, since to do so would involve the contemptible will. The future, then, figures as a kind of negation. It is a cipher or pregnant silence at the core of the laconic Birkin's speech. But this is a less noxious form of nothingness than Gerald's will to power, which in its brutal dominion represents the death drive turned outwards.

Though Gerald exists like a zombie, he cannot bear the thought of death. For those who live by the will alone, mortality is a denial of self-mastery and hence an intolerable insult. The dispossessed can die with less sense of outrage, since they have little enough left to lose; whereas those who bind themselves to the world by power and possession make dying almost impossible for themselves. Birkin, by contrast, welcomes death—but death in the metaphorical sense of radical self-abandonment. He does not believe that either self or society can be reformed: instead, in a kind of apocalyptic *jouissance*, it is necessary to let everything go, 'bust it completely', relinquish one's worldly investments along with one's identity. Only through this revolutionary transformation might some new, post-human life come creeping tentatively over the edge of the abyss. 'You've got to learn not-to-be,' Birkin remarks, 'before you can come into being' (ch. 3). And this involves what he calls a kind of 'destructive creation'. If Gerald is life in thrall to death, Birkin hopes to recruit death into the service of the living. Those who look alive but are secretly dead must be countered by those who accept the need for death as a means to living all the more fully.

So there is a good kind of nothingness as well as a bad one. It is not, after all, simply a choice between being and non-being, as the most celebrated quotation in English literature has it, but between one kind of non-being and another. There is the *via negativa* of Birkin, and there is the mode of non-being signified by Gerald—that of those who appear dynamically alive but who are really nihilists of the spirit. They can impress their authority on the world only because they see it as drained of value. Voluntarism and nihilism converge in the image of Gerald Crich. The more he bends the world to his own desire, the more he knocks the stuffing out of it, so that the less capacity it has to enter into dialogue with him. Which means that he ends up with nothing to confirm his own existence. There can be no valid sovereign without an assenting populace. Absolute power is self-undoing: at the peak of its dominion, it is struck impotent. There is a kind non-being at its core which its antagonists can use to bring it low. This is what happens to Othello, in whom Iago implants a dreadful kind of nothingness (unfounded suspicions of sexual infidelity) which will finally destroy him. Today, Islamic terrorism aims to bring down its Western antagonist by conspiring with a self-destructive impulse at its heart. It can rely on the aid of a fifth columnist: the overreaching will of the West itself. The more Western civilization pollutes the planet and breeds poverty and inequality on a global scale, the more credence it lends to its opponents.

Gerald and Birkin are at least as much blood brothers as ideological alternatives. Hence their solemnly ludicrous naked wrestling on the hearthrug. Birkin may be ready to let the world go, but for him it is a world well lost: there is no great sacrifice involved in renouncing a humanity for which one has such misanthropic contempt. His desire for the impersonal and unknown is among other things a fancy way of keeping Ursula at arm's length, as well as a rationalizing of his hatred for women in general. Nor is his readiness to forsake himself easy to distinguish from self-disgust. Ursula calls him foul, perverse, and death-eating. Since this is his lover speaking, one wonders what his enemies have to say of him. It is not true either that death for him is simply an essential transition: on the contrary, his longing for a new world is shot through with a sadistic jubilation in the wrecking of the old.

So there is no clear-cut distinction between a diseased love of death for its own sake, and an embracing of radical self-dispossession as a means to new life. Thanatos is an untrustworthy servant, who is not easily harnessed to strategic goals. Suicide bombers regard their deaths as strategic: there is no reason to assume that they are everywhere in the grip of a festering *amor fati*. Yet the strategic here is not clearly separable from the symbolic, which can be detected as a kind of surplus within it. An al-Qaida pronouncement some time ago warned that 'if you do not stop your injustices, more and more blood will flow', adding that 'You love life, and we love death.' The statement couples Thanatos with a political programme. Terror puts shock and awe to political ends, linking the expressive to the instrumental. Like the work of art in Kant's view of it, it combines the purposeless with the purposive. It is its sheer excessiveness which alerts us to the 'surplus' of the death drive within it. The same goes for state terror, for which power is also both functional and an end in itself. What we call the arrogance of power is a matter of its touchiness and self-importance, its vanity and narcissism, its rage at being worsted or humiliated even when this thwarts no significant goal. Most of those who wield substantial power do so *inter alia* because they relish it, not just to achieve ends they regard as worthwhile. Because power is bound up with identity, it is always likely to be in excess of its specific purposes. Purely instrumental power does not exist.

Genuine martyrs must be careful not to make fetishes of their deaths; but they must equally be wary of treating them merely as a means to an end, thus falling foul of the very instrumental rationality which their action is meant to put into question. To view one's death strategically is not far from seeking to manipulate the future, and is thus part of the logic which helps to prevent that future from arriving. Neither the martyr nor the suicide can determine the consequences of her actions, since she will not be around to shape them. To see death non-strategically, on the other hand, is to risk falling morbidly in love with it. In avoiding a drab utility, it courts the danger of reducing one's death to an exotic *acte gratuit*. It is perilous to think of the fruits of one's actions, and deeply ill-advised not to.

5

The Living Dead

LET us summarize the argument so far. The sacred is a Janus-faced power, at once life-giving and death-dealing, which can be traced all the way from the orgies of Dionysus to the shattering enthralments of the sublime. For late modern civilization, some of its primary incarnations are known as the unconscious, the death drive, or the Real. This monstrous ambivalence, which for the Judaeo-Christian lineage finds its epitome in the holy terror of God, is also to be found at the root of the modern conception of freedom. The absolute notion of freedom, pressed to an extreme limit, involves a form of terror which turns against the finitude of the flesh in the very act of seeking to serve it. Like the tragic protagonist, it glides through some invisible frontier at which its 'everything' collapses into nothing. Yet even this is not an absolute limit. For it is also possible, for those languishing helplessly in the grip of Thanatos, to *will* such nothingness, which is what we know as evil. However, just as there is a 'good' and a 'bad' kind of freedom, so there is a 'good' as well as 'bad' way of willing nothingness. The good way, as we shall see later, is the path of the tragic scapegoat, who manifests a more healing kind of holy terror.

If the word 'evil' is not to be found in the dictionary of political correctness, it is because it is thought to imply a particular theory of wrongdoing, one which regards it as springing from metaphysical rather than historical causes. It is not poor housing and lack of prospects which led you to steal the car, but the eating of an apple long ago. The business of changing the world so as to diminish the causes of crime accordingly gives way to right-wing talk of the obduracy of human nature and the darkness of the human heart. Talk of evil can be left to the neo-Gothic, vampire-crazed young, for whom the word figures as a compliment.

In the so-called war against terror, 'evil' is used to foreclose the possibility of historical explanation. In this sense, it has something like the function of the word 'taste' for the eighteenth century. In the disparagement of rational analysis which it suggests, it reflects something of the fundamentalism it confronts. Explanation is thought to be exculpation. Reasons become excuses. Terrorist assault is just a surreal sort of madness, like someone turning up at a meeting of the finance committee dressed as a tortoise. Like the sublime, it lies beyond all rational figuration. It is true that some Americans reject all attempts to assign a cause to terrorism while claiming in the next breath that it springs from an envy of American freedom. But life is full of contradictions. On this somewhat obtuse theory, to explain why someone behaves as they do is to demonstrate that they could not have acted otherwise, thus absolving them of responsibility. For this extremist brand of ethics, one is either a full-blown determinist or a full-blooded libertarian. It is the latter creed which has helped to consign so many to death row in the United States.

The truth is that unless you act for a reason, your action is irrational and you are probably absolved of blame for it. A being who was truly independent of all conditioning would not be able to act purposefully at all, any more than an angel could mow the lawn. Acting for a reason involves creatively interpreting the forces which bear in upon us, rather than allowing them to smack us around like snooker balls; and such interpretation involves a degree of freedom. It is inadvisable to caricature your enemy as crazy or spurred on by bestial passion, since morally speaking this lets him off the hook. You must decide whether you are going to see him as evil or mad. Unless we can propose some reasons for why people act as they do, we are not speaking of specifically human behaviour at all, and questions of innocence or guilt become accordingly irrelevant. Moral action must be purposive action: we would not call tripping over a stone morally reprehensible, or wax morally indignant over a rumble in the gut. Reasons may be morally repugnant, but actions without them cannot be.

Genuinely believing that your enemy is irrational, as opposed to pretending to do so for propagandist reasons, will almost certainly ensure that you cannot defeat him. You can only defeat an antagonist whose way of seeing things you can make sense of. Some of the British people may have believed that the IRA had no goals other than to maim and slaughter, but British Intelligence took a different view. There is nothing irrational, as opposed to morally repulsive, about killing people to achieve your political ends. It is not on the same level as believing that you are Marie Antoinette.

If one's enemy really is metaphysically evil, then the chances of defeating him look rather poor. Not even the SAS can stand up to Satan. But there is no reason to assume that evil is indeed metaphysical, in the sense of being beyond all historical explanation. An act can be both evil and historically explicable. The well-intentioned liberal is mistaken not to acknowledge this. He or she rejects the term 'evil' because of its luridly sensationalist ring: it sounds like the kind of description of bad behaviour which is intended to demonize the offender. This argument is more convincing if you are thinking about a teenage car thief from a council estate than if you are thinking about Pol Pot. Pol Pot may or may not have been evil, but using the word about him is plainly more than a form of sensationalism. Even if we do not agree with it, it still makes sense, as it would not make sense to use the word 'evil' of Mary Poppins.

Even so, the liberal may be right to withhold the adjective from Pol Pot. But this is not because Pol Pot's actions were historically intelligible. It is because they represented a certain *kind* of immorality, one which perhaps did not delight in destruction simply for its own sake. From this standpoint, Stalin was not evil in the way that the Moors murderers were, even though what he did was a lot worse. Whereas they killed only a handful of people, he murdered millions. But Pol Pot and Stalin butchered people for a purpose, which does not seem to be true of the Moors murderers. They seem to have killed just for the hell of it. If the word 'evil' retains some contemporary force, it is because it enforces this vital distinction, not because it insists on a non-historical view of vicious behaviour. There is no reason to suppose that destruction for the hell of it is free of historical or psychological preconditions.

The evil are not just prepared to wade through blood, but actually relish the prospect. This is a gratifyingly rare phenomenon (in fact, Immanuel Kant considered such 'diabolical' evil to be impossible),[1] though when it does happen it tends, like air crashes, to happen in a big way. We have seen that a will which takes itself to be all-powerful, or which aspires to that condition, tends to wreak an exceptional amount of chaos and misery. This is known today for the most part as US foreign policy. But it is only when we can speak of gratuitously willing such chaos and misery that we can speak of evil. This is not the case with most senior members of the US administration, however repellent some of them may be, as it is similarly not the case with most terrorists. Even so, there is usually something in such power which is self-delighting, sadistically superfluous, maliciously excessive of its purpose.

With fascism, the ratio between strategic and surplus violence decisively alters. Fascism is almost as fascinated by destruction as it is by achievement. There are times when the cry *Long live death!* enthrals it even more than the prospect of a *Reich* without end. Goebbels seems to have believed at one stage that Hitlerism would probably end in catastrophe, but that this was no good reason to disown it. In a carnival of obscene enjoyment the will turns malevolently against itself, falling in love with pure negativity. In the military-industrial complex of Nazi Germany, life was quite literally harnessed to the production of death. According to Gilles Deleuze, a novel by Klaus Mann offers us this typical sample of everyday Nazi discourse: 'Our beloved *Führer* is dragging us towards the shades of darkness and ever-lasting nothingness. How can we poets, we who have a special affinity for darkness and lower depths, not admire him?'[2] It is what Alain Badiou has called a 'nostalgia for the void'.[3] The self-alienation of humanity under fascism, writes Walter Benjamin, 'has reached such a degree that it can experience its own destruction as a pleasure of the first order'.[4]

The nihilist is the supreme artist, conjuring into existence a nothingness so pure that it beggars all other artefacts, with their inevitable blemishes and imperfections. He is a Manichaean, for whom the Creation and the Fall are simultaneous events. To exist is to be disfigured. 'Nothing has killed itself, creation is its wound,' remarks Danton in Büchner's play. This is the elitist, ascetic face of evil, which like absolute freedom is allergic to the intolerable messiness of the material. The more orgiastic face of evil revels in sheer fleshliness, in that materiality drained of meaning of which the ultimate signifier is a corpse. The devil may have the faded grandeur of a fallen angel, but he is also a vulgar cynic. He is a cocky little know-all who has seen through the spurious depth of things to the unbearable banality which underlies them—the mind-wrenching truth that they simply are what they are, and will be so with insufferable monotony for all eternity. If Satan has an aura of high tragedy, he also has the coarse cackle of the professional debunker, seized by a fit of darkly carnivalesque sniggering at the idea that anything human could be worth a bean, or any piece of reality more worthy than any other. He is the ultimate anti-elitist. The infernal levels the world to eternal repetition, like corpses in a concentration camp. Baudelaire finds a smack of such demonic repetition in the cavortings of the commodity.

Evil is a bogus kind of existence which thrives on non-being, since only in the act of destruction can it feel alive. The evil are slaves to the law: it is just that they keep themselves in existence by deflecting its destructiveness on to others, reaping obscene pleasure from their agonies as well as from their own. Stuck fast in the grip of the death drive, the damned delight in their own torments as well as in the afflictions of their prey, since clinging to their agony is their only alternative to annihilation. They are ready to will the monstrous and hellish, the disgusting and excremental, as long as this is the price of feeling alive. They treat themselves as the sadist treats a victim he deliberately keeps alive so as to torture him still further. They spit in the face of salvation because it threatens to deprive them of the frightful *jouissance* which is all that is left for them of human life. This is why they are both wretched and exultant, miserable and mocking. Evil is a kind of cosmic sulking, which as Kierkegaard remarks in *The Sickness unto Death* rages most violently at the thought that its misery might be taken away from it.

Yet at the same time, since existence as such is an outrage to it, it is plunged into despair because it cannot die. As Father Zosima observes in Dostoevsky's *The Brothers Karamazov*, the damned 'demand that there be no God of life, that God destroy himself and all his Creation. And they shall burn everlastingly in the flames of their own hatred, and long for death and non-being. But death shall not be granted them' (bk. 6, ch. 3). The damned cannot die because like Golding's Pincher Martin they are dead already but too arrogant and deluded to admit it. Because, like Gerald Crich, their actual existence is a form of living death, they do not have the inner depth which might allow them to die for real. They do not have enough remnants of identity even to be able to relinquish themselves, and thus to court the hope of being reborn.

The evil are terrified at the prospect of non-being, stuffing the vacuum which is themselves with their own manic will and fundamentalist dogma. They cannot live with the lack which is desire, and destroy those weaker than themselves because they remind them of their own vacuity. Power loathes weakness, since it brings to mind its own frailty. Yet non-being cannot be destroyed, which is why the whole project of trying to dominate it is both interminable and insanely self-defeating. There are always more Jews, Muslims, homosexuals, women, and other apparent non-persons. This is why hell endures for ever and ever. There is always more existence to exterminate, and it is hard to know when the annihilation of nothingness is complete. In any case, laying violent hands on those around you will bring you no nearer to murdering the non-being at your own heart, since without this abyss known as subjectivity you would be nothing in the first place.

The first suicide-bomber novel of English literature, Joseph Conrad's *The Secret Agent*, stages a conflict between what one might call strategic and non-strategic terrorism. Most of the freakish revolutionary types in the story believe in political action as a means to an end, a view which risks making them the mirror-images of their political opponents. This, however, is a belief rejected by the nameless mad Professor, whom the novel describes as 'the perfect anarchist'. Karl Yundt, one of the Professor's terrorist cronies, dreams of a band of men 'strong enough frankly to give themselves the name of destroyers . . . No pity for anything on earth, including themselves, and death enlisted for good and all in the service of humanity' (ch. 3). This toothless, gouty anarchist seeks to tame and harness Thanatos, a project which is far too moderate for the mad Professor.

Yundt's spine-chilling vision betrays an obvious contradiction. If you despise humanity enough to destroy it, in what sense can you do this in the name of humanity? If it is permissible to wipe out great swathes of the species, how can it be worth saving? Yundt speaks of having no pity 'for anything on earth', which presumably must include the oppressed he is supposed to champion. Perhaps he is a kind of Birkin, who wants to annihilate humanity in its present form for the sake of an improved future version of it. One is reminded of Bertolt Brecht's sardonic proposal to dissolve the existing people and elect another one. But where would a future humanity spring from, if not from the present? If this regenerated humanity is not somehow inherent in the actual, then how can we speak of the future as *our* future? Have we not been replaced rather than reformed?

The Professor differs from his anarchist colleagues in yearning for a revolutionary act which would be utterly unblemished. As such, it would need to be untainted by the interests and desires which drive on the other revolutionaries in the novel. For these 'pathological' emotions leash you to the very situation you hope to abolish. An entirely pure act would need to be without motive altogether. Like God's creation, it would have to be performed just for the hell of it. Yet then there is no more reason to do it than not to do it. This is why there must be an inevitable obscurity about the Professor, whose will is so absolute that it is resolute for no reason at all. He, too, wants to exterminate humanity, but he is neither illogical nor sentimental enough to wish to do this in humanity's name. As a member of the spiritual elect of evil, who resemble their virtuous counterparts in their rejection of utility, the Professor despises politics, regards himself as absolved from social and political convention, and feels nothing but contempt for the common people. 'They depend on life,' he observes, '. . . a complex, organized fact open to attack at every point; whereas I depend on death, which knows no restraint and cannot be attacked. My superiority is evident' (ch. 4).

By embracing death, the Professor is insulated from time, change, history, and decay, living a sterile, exultant existence of absolute freedom. If he cannot be destroyed, it is in a sense because he is dead already. He has all the invulnerability to assault of sheer negation. The Professor is one of the living dead, and is gleefully proud of the fact. Any two-bit citizen can live, but it requires a certain majesty to move habitually in the domain of the deceased. This perfect anarchist has attained the absolute freedom of a cypher, which any specific action or desire could only contaminate. The price of his freedom is thus total impotence. Like a modernist work of art, he has shaken off the material world and achieved an autonomy so pure that you can stare right through it. Nobody, quite literally, can touch him: as he stalks through the streets of London he grasps in his pocket a small India-rubber ball, which is connected to an explosive device strapped to his body. This, the narrator remarks, is the 'supreme guarantee of his sinister freedom'. His invulnerability lies not just in the fact that he cannot be arrested, but that by being prepared to blow himself into eternity at any moment, he has achieved a freedom which is at once empty and absolute.

As such, the Professor is in and out of time simultaneously. In this, he resembles the Romantic or modernist work of art, which is a wedge of eternity within secular time, the meeting-point of the finite and the infinite. The scene of the anarchist outrage in the novel is Greenwich Observatory, marker of the prime meridian and still point of the turning world. The Professor himself has no truck with time, narrative, or history. He signifies that deathly impulse within them which negates their forward motion, causing them to roll backwards or implode on themselves. 'You revolutionaries,' he upbraids his colleagues in language which could be Birkin's, '. . . plan the future, you lose yourselves in reveries of economical systems derived from what is; whereas what's wanted is a clean sweep and a clear start for a new conception of life' (ch. 4). It is the familiar cry of the avant-gardist, who rather than submit to the messiness of history and material process seeks to leap at a bound from present to future, actual to desirable, finite to infinite. One squeeze of his India-rubber ball and the Professor will catapult himself at a stroke from time to eternity. He will thus act out in the flesh what he is already in the spirit.

Yet every such fantasy contains a flaw, and in the Professor's case it lies in his inability to come up with the perfect detonator. The one he has leaves a frustrating twenty-second gap between being activated and going off. There is no instant self-consignment to eternity. If you can dream of one, it is only because you are careless of the fact that others will have to pick up the bits and pieces of your supposedly flawless action. That it will have no consequences for you does not mean that it will have no consequences at all. There are those in the novel whose task is to pick up the tell-tale bits and pieces of the mentally defective child Stevie, who is blown to bits by the terrorists. Actions cannot be pure, because they have effects which are in principle incalculable. Matter cannot be annihilated: it can be recycled from one form to another, but it cannot be expunged, and will come oozing over the edges of the black hole you try to blow in it. There can be no absolutely original future, since any imaginable future must be fashioned out of the tainted materials of the present.

The Professor is among other things a parody of a modernist artist: elitist, anti-bourgeois, beyond good and evil, gazing down upon a degenerate time from the Olympian standpoint of eternity. He is a demonic version of the angelic Stevie, another of the novel's mad artists, who scribbles endless circles which suggest 'a rendering of cosmic chaos, the symbolism of a mad art attempting the inconceivable' (ch. 3). Because he is absolved from time, the Professor is unable to act, since time is the medium in which action unfolds. To act is to objectify yourself as a free subject, but for the Professor, who represents pure bodiless subjectivity, such objectivation signifies death. This, however, is of no great moment, since as a nihilist in love with extinction he wants to blow up not just this or that piece of reality, but reality as such. He thus poses the greatest possible danger to the state, and no danger whatsoever. He is an antagonist of everything and a threat to nothing. The closest he can come to extinguishing the whole world is extinguishing himself. As with traditional evil, the Professor's real adversary is the material world itself. Matter is the stuff which besmirches his fantasies of omnipotence. It is creation which the Professor finds intolerable, and which he dreams of countering with the equally ecstatic act of destruction.

This is why he loiters constantly on the brink of action without ever taking the plunge, toying with his India-rubber ball without actually pressing it. Absolute freedom flourishes only in this twilight zone, in the no-man's-land between decision and execution. As a liminal figure poised between life and death, time and eternity, the Professor cannot act because the absolute will he represents can see action only as self-loss. Which indeed, in his case, squeezing his detonator would literally be. The perfect act is impossible because it cannot help leaving a residue: it needs a fleshly incarnation in some objective stuff, but this means that the very medium of such action is also its undoing. This deadly dream of purity cannot stomach the fact that human beings are subjects and objects at the same time, creatures who move on the rough ground rather than on pure ice, and who like the Professor's defective detonator can never fully coincide with themselves.

Though Stevie is blown to pieces at Greenwich Observatory, we do not actually see this happen. This is not just a matter of decorum. Several of the most central events in Conrad's fiction are squinted at sideways rather than seen head-on, or reported by one or more intermediary. Lord Jim's jump from his ship is one such non-event, but so in *The Secret Agent* is the killing of Verloc by his long-suffering wife. These are decisive moments, crises or epiphanies of the subject which defeat representation. Mrs Verloc's act of stabbing her husband suggests that she has momentarily broken through her customary false consciousness for a Kurtz-like insight into the authentic horror of things; but we are not allowed access to her consciousness at this moment, since how such radical change is possible in a world of strict causality and temporal continuity is as unthinkable as the

Kantian *noumenon*. Like a Dadaist happening, such an act simply is what it is, absolved from rhyme or reason.

Truly free actions, those which like Winnie Verloc's spring from the very nucleus of the self, are sublime. To make a graven image of them would be to reduce their mysterious elusiveness to a determinate formula, and thus to nullify them. The authentic self is present only as a kind of absence or oversight. Freedom can be shown but not said. The price you pay for a liberty beyond all limit is eternal silence. Transformations of the self are real enough, but how they come about in such a sluggish, deterministic, grossly material world must remain an enigma. In this sense, *The Secret Agent* connives in its formal strategies with the Professor's view of the world, much as it detests him. It, too, is appalled by the vista of a material world stretching to infinity in all directions. Conrad, like his Professor, is an elitist modernist artist with a low opinion of the masses. The indestructibility of the everyday, its stolid persistence in its own dull, self-deluded being, is in one sense as repugnant to the novel as it is to the Professor. Verloc is so obese that how he moves at all is a mystery. Yet in another sense this recalcitrance is all that stands between us and the horror of absolute freedom. Better an infinite continuum of meaningless matter than an apocalyptic break. London cannot be destroyed, but only because it is a great desert of inorganic matter, a slimy aquarium enveloped in murky dampness. *The Secret Agent* thus satirizes the commonplace petty-bourgeois world, while exploiting its very commonplaceness to discredit those out to devastate it. The anarchists are to be feared—but they are also pathetic. This is both our comfort and our terror.

At the end of the novel, 'the incorruptible Professor walked . . . averting his eyes from the odious multitude of mankind. He had no future. He disdained it. He was a force. His thoughts caressed the images of ruin and destruction. He walked frail, insignificant, shabby, miserable—and terrible in the simplicity of his idea calling madness and despair to the regeneration of the world. Nobody looked at him. He passed on unsuspected and deadly, like a pest in the street full of men' (ch. 13). Yet this is not the only image of horror in Conrad's text. What is equally chilling is the fact that it is state authority, in the person of Mr Vladimir, which is egging the anarchists on for its own devious political ends. And the British state colludes in its own way with this foreign-sponsored terror. It is, as one British Minister puts it, a question of 'authorized scoundrelism'. The law itself is in cahoots with criminality. Anarchist and police inspector are pawns in the same game, each fully apprised of which moves are permissible and which are not. 'The terrorist and the policeman both come from the same basket' (ch. 3), comments the Professor, whose aim is to break this complicity by transcending the social game altogether. 'The mind and instincts of a burglar,' remarks the Chief Inspector, 'are of the same kind as the mind and instincts of a police officer' (ch. 4). Robbing a bank and founding one are kindred practices. The law protects us from the unspeakable, but in its paranoid violence helps to bring it on. That there is something mad about the law is a common-place of post-structuralism; but it is a rather more persuasive proposition when it flows, as here, from the pen of an author who was a rabid opponent of political radicalism and a passionate devotee of social order.

6

Scapegoats

THE idea of sacrifice is not in the least glamorous these days. It is what mothers do for their loutish sons, harassed wives for their imperious husbands, and working-class soldiers for pampered politicians. Sacrifice is the clarion call of the fascist Fatherland, with its necrophiliac rites and ceremonials of self-oblation. In religious cultures, it is a violent procedure for placating a savage god, offering him bribes in the hope that you will be spared his wrath. It smacks of a morbid cult of self-abnegation, as its victims come to revel in their own powerlessness and rub their meekness aggressively in others' faces.

The idea of sacrifice has a quaintly archaic ring to it, though it is in fact as much a modern as an ancient practice. Modernity has its sacred rituals as much as antiquity. For the ideology of progress, for example, past and present must be immolated on the altar of the future. Present gratification must be offered up in the name of the future, and history is the term for this endless postponement. In this secularized theodicy, destruction, in the form of the repudiation of the past, is to be affirmed as the harbinger of creation. As in traditional sacrifice, good may be plucked from evil: Kant argues in his *Idea for a Universal History* that war strengthens political states, and thus is ultimately conducive to peace; that mutual antagonism makes for peaceable progress; and that violence and chaos are ultimately beneficial since they persuade us to submit to the rule of law. Max Weber thought that the idea of infinite progress had struck death meaningless, since it was now no more than an essential transition to the eternal life of the future.

On the whole, however, modernity has regarded the self as too precious to be abandoned. If sacrifice blurs the bounds between life and death, conditions which most pre-modern cultures know to be on the most intimate of terms with each other, the modern will enforces an absolute distinction between them. Modernity regards self-dispossession as the enemy of self-realization, not as its vital precondition, and so tends to buy its self-realization on the cheap. Postmodernity is equally sceptical of sacrifice, largely because it is uncertain that there is enough of a self to be relinquished in the first place.

To propose that sacrifice can be a radical notion may seem a piece of perversity. Yet it is not so outlandish a proposition as it may seem. Giving things up, after all, is not always dourly life-denying. Political revolutionaries quite often sacrifice their happiness and well-being, but in the name of a richer existence for all. There is a kind of asceticism which is in the cause of abundance. The word 'sacrifice' literally means 'to make sacred'. Sacrificial rituals involve taking some humble or worthless piece of life and converting it into something special and potent. In order to pass from the one condition to the other, however, the thing in question has to pass through a process of death and dissolution—one which, like Oedipus at Colonus or the mad Lear on the heath, renders it well-nigh unrecognizable. The idea of sacrifice is not hospitable to notions of piecemeal reform. Sacrifice concerns the passage of the reviled thing from humiliation to power. It is what the philosopher Georges Bataille calls 'creation by means of loss'.[1]

Sacrifice thus has the inner structure of the tragic. But it is tragic, too, in the sense that it is both pitiful and fearful that it should prove necessary in the first place. A just society would require no such radical self-dissolution. A condition which cannot be repaired without so extreme a *kenosis* must be dire indeed. That a decent human dispensation demands not only amending the *ancien régime*, but dying to it, is a symptom of historical crisis, not a piece of macabre self-indulgence. In this sense, those who reject the idea of sacrifice are those who place their faith in eternal life—in that perpetual version of the present known as the future. It is this complacent continuum which the act of sacrifice ruptures.

In pre-modern societies, the sacrificial victim is usually a hideous, mutilated creature. It acts as a scapegoat on to which the community can project its own violence and criminality, and in doing so can disavow them. The scapegoat is driven beyond the boundaries of the city, to suffer an ignominious death beyond its walls. By this ritual mechanism, the people cleanse themselves of pollution and guilt. Sacrifice is needed when the community falls sick; but the community is always sick. This seems to have been the point of the annual ritual of Thargelia in ancient Athens, in which the pollution which the city had accumulated over the previous year was ceremonially purged. To accomplish this, two human scapegoats were selected from the most wretched and destitute of the population, occasionally recruited from the local gaols. One could be a professional scapegoat in ancient Athens, rather as one can be a professional scrounger today. The positive aspect of the job was that you were fed and accommodated for nothing and treated as playing a vital role in the city's regeneration; the negative aspect was that you were treated with revulsion and contempt, and perhaps in early times even murdered. In the end, it was not a profession with a great deal of job satisfaction.

Housed and fed a special diet at the city's expense, the sacrificial scapegoats were then paraded through the streets, struck on the genitals with herbaceous plants, and run out of town. The city could then settle down again to the business of lying, cheating, murdering, and blaspheming until the next Thargelia came round. But it kept a supply of scapegoats on stand-by for times of crisis, as a modern city keeps emergency services in reserve. If a calamity such as a famine or foreign invasion befell

Athens, the scapegoats could be rolled out like sponges to soak up the resultant impurities. Like all sacred things, the scapegoat is both holy and cursed, since the more polluted it becomes by absorbing the city's impurities, the more redemption it brings to it. The redemptive victim is the one who takes a general hurt into its own body, and in doing so transforms it into something rich and rare.

In this politically institutionalized version of sacrifice, the scapegoat maintains a metaphorical rather than metonymic relation to the people as a whole. It is a substitute for them, rather than a signifying part of their collective life. Far from glimpsing a reflection of its own features in this traumatic horror, the community thrusts it out, thus disavowing its significance and perpetuating its own self-blindness. By displacing its own deformities on to a vilified other, it can rid itself magically of its defects. Sacrifice of this sort is a kind of social therapy or public hygiene, from which you emerge cleaner and stronger. But there is another reading of sacrifice in which the scapegoat is not metaphorical of the people, but metonymic of them. It is a piece of them, rather than a displacement. In this torn, twisted thing, the people come to acknowledge something of their own collective disfigurement, contemplating themselves in the Real rather than the imaginary. They recognize in this derelict being their own horrific double, and in doing so open themselves to a deathliness at the core of their own identity. We ourselves are monstrous because as creatures who are both beasts and non-beasts, godlike and ungodly, inside yet askew to the social order, and (as in incest) capable of playing several roles simultaneously, we garble vital distinctions simply by existing. The point of recognizing this indiscriminate state is not to see through cultural differences, but to acknowledge something of their arbitrariness and fragility.

This obscene creature, the people confess, was cast out of the city not because it was too foreign but because it was too close to the bone. Conjugating Aristotle's twin tragic responses of pity and fear, they come to feel compassion for what petrifies them. In gathering the unclean thing to themselves, welcoming the sublimely terrible other, the people symbolically mark the extreme limit of their own form of life. For if that form of life survives only by its violent exclusion of this monster of dispossession, then it would take more than some liberal or postmodern 'inclusivity' to accommodate it. Only by passing through death and self-dissolution can the social order come to regard this frightful Real as friendly. Sacrifice is thus a symbolic form of social revolution. What is rejected becomes the corner-stone. In the strange homeopathy of the scapegoat, poison is converted to cure. We are dealing here with what Alain Badiou calls 'the invention of a language wherein folly, scandal, and weakness supplant knowing, reason, order, and power, and wherein non-being is the only legitimisable affirmation of being . . .'[2] It is the language neither of business executives nor of the orthodox left.

Sacrifice can also take a eucharistic form, in which the act of identifying with the abject creature takes the dramatically literal form of eating it. A polluted piece of matter is converted into the *praxis* of a human meal, and the participants proclaim their shared life with one other through the medium of this monstrosity. Where they once encountered each other on the ground of the symbolic or the imaginary, now they can establish those more durable relations which pass through the Real. Eating is itself a matter of life and death, since to consume the victim is both to draw life from it and to destroy it. New life is possible only if one's current form of existence goes under with the victim which signifies it.

There is, then, a 'good' kind of nothingness—one to be glimpsed in the potentially fertile non-being of the dispossessed, rather than in the sterile negativity of the will which subjugates them. Lear is wrong to suppose that nothing can come of nothing. In confronting the maimed and mutilated scape-goat, an encounter which involves opening itself to its own misshapenness, the community is offered a chance to press this deathly negativity into the service of more abundant life. Only by embracing the inhuman can it discover its own humanity. It is this which Theseus is called upon to do, when he stands before the broken, blinded Oedipus in Sophocles's drama *Oedipus at Colonus*. As Oedipus himself once returned an answer to the riddle of the hybrid Sphinx, so his monstrously defiling presence now poses a question to the city of Athens. Is it to take him in, or cast him out as so much dangerously polluted garbage? Rather as Oedipus himself recognized the image of the human in the misshapen Sphinx, declaring 'Man' to be the solution to its conundrum, so Athens is now being asked to recognize the image of the human in this deformed creature on its threshold. If it takes him in, power will flow from his weakness: the outcast king will be raised up as a god to protect the city from harm. What was once too lowly to be represented will become too sublime to be so.

If previously Oedipus stood for a kind of death in life, now he will prove a source of life in death. Only a life which has passed through death, which is the meaning of 'sacred', has the transformative force which the city needs. To embrace the deathly Oedipus is to recognize that there is a way of acclaiming non-being which is life-giving rather than nihilistic. 'I am made a man in the hour when I cease to be?' (or perhaps, 'Am I to be counted as something only when I am reduced to nothing?'), the blind king cries out. Theseus takes him into the city—an action, one might add, of which the contemporary West has so far failed to find an equivalent in its own dealings with the foreign menace. It is unable to decipher the symptoms of weakness and despair in the raging fury at its gate, and thus is capable only of fear, rather than of pity for the injustices which brought this monster to birth. Today, the scapegoat or *pharmakos* is neither a burnt offering nor a couple of recruited gaolbirds, but the wretched of the earth, the garbage of global capitalism.

Oedipus is himself a *pharmakos*—at once sovereign and out-law, sacred and sinful, guilty and innocent, poison and cure, blessed and cursed. Just as the sovereign inspires both awe and affection, so the outcast must be pitied as well as feared. The destiny of the city is bound up with both figures: both are repre-sentative of the people, the one formally, the other unofficially, and both therefore have the sacred power to transfigure their lives. Oedipus is cursed because, like all sacrificial scapegoats, he is 'made sin' for the people, forced to symbolize their collec-tive guilt and crime; yet he is holy because he is thereby the scene of the city's potential transformation. 'I come to offer you a gift—my tortured body—a sorry sight,' he cries, 'but there is value in it more than beauty.'

The scapegoat has been described as a 'guilty innocent'[3]—an appropriate term for the likes of Oedipus, who has committed the most abominable transgressions without knowing what he was doing. For Emmanuel Levinas, simply to be a subject is to exist in this oxymoronic state, summoned into existence by the traumatizing, accusatory demand of the other, and responsible for this other as the very condition of one's own subjecthood. Scapegoats are innocent in the sense that they have committed no deliberate personal offence, but guilty in the sense that they bear the offences of others. They bear them most importantly in the sense that these wrongs are done *to* them, so that they present a living image of injustice. In their own wretchedness, they represent a general condition.

The scapegoat is the one who brings this condition (what St John calls the 'sin of the world', as opposed to this or that individual transgression) into the most intense focus, since it is its most vulnerable victim. It marks the place where this dehumanization is most purely distilled, which is what is 'guilty' about this innocent. As such, it shows up the weakness of power—its anxiety and neurotic compulsion, its pathological lust for a victim—and in doing so reveals something of the power of weakness. It is the mangled bodies of those upon whom power weighs most heavily which offer the most eloquent testimony to its bankruptcy. In this sense, too, the outcast is the inverted truth of the sovereign. Moreover, if the sovereign is powerful because he can rise no higher, the outcast represents that parody of power which springs from knowing that you can fall no further.

To call the scapegoat a guilty innocent is to say that it shows up the violence done to it as structural—as a common condition rather than a personal flaw. The scapegoat is not individually responsible for this state of affairs, but it is bound up with it all the same, and provides its most graphic icon. Like Oedipus, it is subjectively blameless but objectively contaminated. The woe-scarred, prematurely aged children of Blake and Dickens, innocent in themselves yet the most poignant signs of a more general exploitation, are guilty innocents in just this sense. The scapegoat is 'guilty' because as a sign of the dispossessed, it bears the burden of this warped condition; but since it is also 'innocent', with no vested interests in maintaining this state of affairs and with every incentive to abolish it, it marks the place of its potential transformation. The state of guilty innocence comes about when one is both victim and agent—when the 'guilty' victim itself becomes the 'innocent' agent of its own metamorphosis. And since the scapegoat's specific plight cannot be repaired without a general refashioning, its irreducibly particular existence shows up its situation to be a universal one. Its very existence is a negative index of transformation, since any change which did not dissolve its own existence would necessarily be inadequate. The only change which matters is one which would do away with the scapegoat itself. But since this capability is in its own hands, in the modern political world if not in ancient ritual, the scapegoat does away with itself by the act of coming to power. It is this process of coming to power that we call sacrifice.

The scapegoat is anonymous because it signifies more than itself; but it is also dehumanized because there is something inhuman about the purely human state to which it has been reduced. If that state is terrible to look upon, it is because men and women need the decent drapery of culture if they are to find their own and each other's presence tolerable. Only when humanity is invested with specific cultural features can it be regarded without horror. Since human beings perpetually exceed themselves in the surplus known as culture, they become inhuman when they are stripped to no more than themselves. In the repellent figure of the *pharmakos*, human existence itself appears a scandal and obscenity. Pressed to an extreme, humanity shows up both as purely itself and not itself at all. Yet it is this stark, unhoused condition which has to be salvaged. And this is possible only by an answerable sort of inhumanity, one which is able to encounter others on the ground of the Real.

World literature is strewn with scapegoats. It is full of doubled, ambiguous creatures who are both holy and reviled, cursed and life-giving. Sophocles's Philoctetes is one such *pharmakos*, a howling, pus-ridden castaway whose rotting body has the sacred power to bring about human reconciliation.[4] Another lies at the centre of what has a claim to be the greatest English novel, and is certainly the longest. The virtuous young heroine of Samuel Richardson's *Clarissa* is pursued by the aristocratic rake Lovelace, and having been tricked away from her home is imprisoned, tormented, drugged, and raped. But Lovelace is cheated of his triumph as his victim deliberately appropriates her own death, withdrawing her body ceremonially from a social order which can treat it only as sexual or economic property. Clarissa Harlowe is the greatest *pharmakos* of English litera-ture—an abused woman of outstanding kindliness and intelli-gence who is made to suffer at the hands of an obnoxiously patriarchal society. Her family treat her as a pawn in the marriage-and-property game; and in refusing this game absolutely, Clarissa is turning her back among other things on the abiding motifs of the English novel.[5]

At the heart of the English Enlightenment, then, with its robust faith in reason and progress, we stumble upon a modern crucifixion, as Clarissa becomes a sign of all the torn, discarded victims of a social order obsessed with property and power. She is the prototypical 'guilty innocent' of English literature, afflicted as she is by the unwarranted guilt of the raped woman. This guilt is a kind of original sin: you were not responsible for the crime, but you brought it about simply by existing. Clarissa is plagued by anxieties that she may have led Lovelace on. She finds her seducer sexually attractive, and has rather too smug a faith in her ability to domesticate him. She is, in a word, no Little Nell. The reader, at least, can be thankful for that. If she is a sacrificial victim, she is by no means a spotless one. Indeed, her (mostly male) critics have vilified her as dull, naive, priggish, prudish, morbid, perverse, inflexible, masochistic, narcissistic, self-pitying, self-deceived, and sanctimonious.

Clarissa is indeed morbid, perverse, inflexible, narcissistic, and masochistic, which is part of what is so commendable about her. After the traumatic encounter with the Real which is her rape, she refuses to re-enter the symbolic order of English middle-class society, speaks of her herself as 'nothing', and declares that 'I am nobody's'. She demonstrates this refusal of proprietorship in the most dramatic way possible, by transporting her body out of harm's way into death. In this predatory environment, the only way to safeguard the self is to lose it. The dying Clarissa is nothing, errant, schizoid, a non-person and empty place. If she is perversely absolute for death, living as she does under the tutelage of Thanatos, it is because she has recognized well enough that this is no society for a woman to live in.

Rather than die in a decorous, hole-in-the-corner fashion, she puts her dying brazenly on public show, converting her violated body into a political theatre. In performing her death like a martyr, she constructs her own public sphere and turns the tables with agreeable sadism on her remorseful rapist and horror-stricken relatives. The sacrificial victim thus turns its weakness into power. If she is perverse and narcissistic, it is because she refuses with admirable obstinacy to be deflected from the self-absorbed business of her dying, leaving those around her with blood on their hands. In yielding herself up to the morbid pleasures of the death drive, drawing secret delight from the process of her own dissolution, part of Clarissa's 'obscene enjoyment' lies in bringing her victors low. There is a similar ambiguity about some of Henry James's passive–aggressive heroines. To call Clarissa's death a kind of victory is not to advance it as a paradigm of political action, or to indulge in some morbid cult of victimage. It is to commend her for salvaging value from an event which should never have happened in the first place.

Richardson's heroine is, as Samuel Johnson famously complained, 'an unconscionable time a-dying'; indeed, in an astonishing subversion of literary realism, about one-third of this million-word novel is taken up with Clarissa's meticulous preparations for her own extinction. But this is the point. It would be far too convenient for the social order which has hounded her to death to have her expire modestly sequestered from the public gaze. Clarissa's death is a gesture of political disengagement—a surreal act of resignation from a power-structure which she has seen through, and one made all the more sweetly devastating by its unfailing meekness and courtesy. By scripting her own death so punctiliously, she makes of it an event in her life rather than simply the end-point of it. The novel plucks from her dying an implicitly political statement, converting its heroine's manhandled body into an image of solidarity with all those who have been plundered of themselves. Clarissa is a scapegoat not simply because she is a victim—by no means all victims are scapegoats—but because she becomes in that condition the nodal-point or icon of a more general regime of injustice, signifying in her 'polluted' condition the monstrosity which must be confronted if the social order is to be remade. Since the woman is both integral to that order and reviled by it, no more graphic image of the liminal *pharmakos* could be found.

Modern-minded critics, who find talk of sacrifice, masochism, pollution, and the death-drive either distressingly morbid or embarrassingly archaic, have branded Clarissa a prude because she values her chastity over life itself. The case is more accurate than it knows. Clarissa does indeed prize her honour and chastity more than life itself, which is what is so scandalous about her. The honour she prizes so dearly is that thing in her which is more than herself—that demand for respect and recognition without which life is mere biological duration. What is radical about this heroine is the fact that she refuses to live on such compromised terms. In the absence of her ultimate object of desire, she is not prepared to be fobbed off with shoddy substitutes for it. By sacrificing her very existence to this precious kernel of selfhood, yielding up her life for her desire, she dies to preserve her identity rather than to destroy it. It is this which makes her a martyr rather than a suicide.

For much of the novel, Clarissa is already one of the living dead, her whole existence a kind of aftermath. She is the English Antigone, who like Sophocles's heroine refuses all compromise with the powers of this world, and must therefore court accusations of being stubborn, perverse, and self-admiring. It is simply that the burial upon which Clarissa insists, unlike Antigone, is her own rather than someone else's. The ruling powers can see both women only as stubborn little minxes who shut their ears to reason. Both protagonists are mute testimony to the fact that a just civilization, paradoxically, could be founded only upon this clenched, solitary, unsociable fidelity to truth, one which will bring the witness herself no worldly gain. The tragedy is that desire is now so caught up with property and contaminated by power that only death can transcend this diseased condition. Richardson, with something of his own heroine's obdurate perversity, fails to ride to Clarissa's rescue and refuses his distraught readers a happy ending. Instead, he insists on treating the questions he has raised realistically—which is to say, pressing them all the way through into full-blooded tragedy. That *Clarissa* is one of the very few tragic novels in English before Thomas Hardy is testimony enough to his courage.

We have been investigating in the course of this study two opposed figures of the living dead. There are martyrs like Clarissa, who embrace non-being in the name of a more flourishing kind of existence; and there are those vampiric creatures like Lawrence's Gerald Crich, who batten on non-being as an ersatz form of life. When men and women come to crave such negativity as a life-saving drug, ransacking others to lay their hands on it, we may legitimately speak of evil. Tragedy at its most searching is a reminder that those forms of life which fear the monstrous lack of being at their own heart will tend to discover an image of this frightful Real in some hideous, misshapen creature who must be banished from their gates. In our own world, one consequence of that disavowal is known as terrorism. The terrorist is not the *pharmakos*; but he is created by it, and can only be defeated when justice is done to it. We may end, then, with the words with which Raymond Williams concluded his *Culture and Society 1780–1950*:[6]

There are ideas, and ways of thinking, with the seeds of life in them, and there are others, perhaps deep in our minds, with the seeds of a general death. Our measure of success in recognizing these kinds, and in naming them making possible their common recognition, may be literally the measure of our future.

Notes

PREFACE

1. Since someone is mathematically certain to perpetrate the joke 'Holy Terry', I hereby issue a spoiler.

I. INVITATION TO AN ORGY

1. René Girard has some illuminating remarks on the levelling nature of Dionysus in his *Violence and the Sacred* (London and New York, 2005), ch. 5.

2. The concept is pervasive throughout Žižek's work; but see, for example, *The Sublime Object of Ideology* (London, 1989), Part 3.

3. G. W. F. Hegel, *Phenomenology of Spirit* (Oxford, 1977), 19.

4. R. P. Winnington-Ingram, *Euripides and Dionysus* (Cambridge, 1997), 144.

5. Euripides, *The Bacchae and Other Plays* (Harmondsworth, 1973), 207.

6. Those postmodern thinkers for whom all hierarchies are objectionable should recall Hannah Arendt's claim in *The Origins of Totalitarianism* that Stalinism and Nazism were radically anti-hierarchical systems. Power was not scrupulously gradated but invested wholly in the Leader, to whom all other citizens then stood in a formally equal relationship. Not all egalitarianism is progressive.

7. William Empson, *Some Versions of Pastoral* (London, 1966), 14. This, in effect, is Empson's version of Freud, to which he gives the name of pastoral.

8. One attempt to anchor reason in the senses is known as the aesthetic, which aims for a kind of concrete rationality or rigorous logic of perception. See my *The Ideology of the Aesthetic* (Oxford, 1990), ch. 1.

9. See R. P. Winnington-Ingram, *Euripides and Dionysus* (Cambridge, 1997), 57.

10. The play is translated by Martin Greenberg in *Heinrich von Kleist: Five Plays* (New Haven and London, 1988).

11. I have dealt with these matters more fully in my study *Sweet Violence: The Idea of the Tragic* (Oxford, 2003).

12. *The Confessions of St Augustine* (London, 1963), 72.

13. Quoted by Luke Gibbons, *Edmund Burke and Ireland* (Cambridge, 2003), 134.

14. See Alain Badiou, *L'Être et l'événement* (Paris, 1988). See also the excellent study by Peter Hallward, *Badiou: A Subject to Truth* (Minneapolis and London, 2003), Part 2, 5.

15. The Pharisees have a remote affinity with modern Islamic radicals, both groups being militantly anti-colonialist but also theocratic, aiming to replace a secular colonial power with a purified religious state.

16. Friedrich Nietzsche, *The Will to Power* (New York, 1968), 404.

2. STATES OF SUBLIMITY

1. I have treated Burke's views on these matters more fully in *Heathcliff and the Great Hunger* (London, 1995), ch. 2.

2. Rene Girard, *Violence and the Sacred* (London and New York, 2005), 267.

3. For an excellent study of Burke, colonialism, and the sublime, see Luke Gibbons, *Edmund Burke and Ireland* (Cambridge, 2003).

4. Slavoj Žižek, *For They Know Not What They Do* (London, 1991), 30.

5. Edmund Burke, *Reflections on the Revolution in France*, in L. G. Mitchell (ed.), *The Writings and Speeches of Edmund Burke* (Oxford, 1989), viii. 129. An illuminating account of Burke's notions of sublimity is to be found in Tom Furniss, *Edmund Burke's Aesthetic Ideology* (Cambridge, 1993), Part 2, ch. 5.

6. There is even a stage beyond this catatonia: that of the so-called *Muselmann* of the Nazi death camps, over whom the law and ideology no longer have a hold, and on whom they no longer even place demands, since there is no subjectivity left to be commanded, inspired, deceived, or cajoled. See Giorgio Agamben, *Homer Sacer: Sovereign Power and Bare Life* (Stanford, 1998), and *States of Exception* (Chicago, 2005).

7. Michel Foucault famously questions this notion of power as negative, insisting instead that it can be positive. But he does not claim that the law can be *morally* positive.

8. Franco Moretti, *Modern Epic* (London, 1996), 25.

9. *Marx and Engels on Literature and Art* (Moscow, 1976), 83.

10. I have investigated these issues further in *The English Novel: An Introduction* (Oxford, 2004).

11. Quoted in Franco Moretti, *The Way of the World* (London, 1987), 102.

12. David Hume, *Treatise of Human Nature* (Oxford, 1960), 566.

13. R. B. MacDowell (ed.), *The Writings and Speeches of Edmund Burke* (Oxford, 1991), ix. 614.

14. Blaise Pascal, *Pensées* (Harmondsworth, 1966), 46–7.

15. See Hans Reiss (ed.), *Kant: Political Writings* (Cambridge, 1970), 143.

16. Quoted by Keith Ansell Pearson, *Nietzsche* (London, 2005), 55.

3. FEAR AND FREEDOM

1. F. W. J. Schelling, *System of Transcendental Idealism* (Charlottesville, Va., 1978), 35.

2. Ibid. 34.

3. G. W. F. Hegel, *Phenomenology of Spirit* (Oxford, 1977), 360.

4. Ibid. 362.

5. Schiller's notion of the aesthetic turns on such a suspension of actuality in the name of perpetual possibility. See Friedrich Schiller, *On the Aesthetic Education of Man* (Oxford, 1967).

6. G. W. F. Hegel, *Phenomenology of Spirit* (Oxford, 1977), 362.

7. Ibid. 261.

8. See my *The Ideology of the Aesthetic* (Oxford, 1990).

4. SAINTS AND SUICIDES

1. Slavoj Žižek, *Tarrying with the Negative* (London, 2003), 222.

2. Quoted by Alenka Zupanicic, *Ethics of the Real* (London, 2000), 1.

3. See Alain Badiou, *Saint Paul: The Foundation of Universalism* (Stanford, Calif., 2003).

4. Arthur Schopenhauer, *The World as Will and Representation* (New York, 1969), i. 196.

5. THE LIVING DEAD

1. Almost all accounts of evil nowadays confine themselves almost entirely to two topics: Kant and the Holocaust. The present account hopes to be more diverse.

2. Quoted in Gilles Deleuze, *A Thousand Plateaus* (London, 1988), 231.

3. Quoted in Peter Hallward, *Badiou: A Subject to Truth* (Minneapolis and London, 2003), 263. I have discussed the question of evil more fully in *Sweet Violence: The Idea of the Tragic* (Oxford, 2003), ch. 9.

4. Walter Benjamin, *Illuminations* (London, 1973), 244.

6. SCAPEGOATS

1. Georges Bataille, *Visions of Excess: Selected Writings 1927–1939* (Minneapolis, 1985), 120.

2. Alain Badiou, *Saint Paul: The Foundation of Universalism* (Stanford, 2003), 47.

3. See Paul Ricœur, *The Symbolism of Evil* (Boston, 1969), 225.

4. Two modern scapegoats also spring to mind: Heathcliff in *Wuthering Heights*, described as 'a gift of God: though it's as dark almost as if it came from the devil', who lives with the unflinching absolutism of Thanatos, refuses to back down on the Real of his implacable desire for Catherine, and is borne by it straight into death; and Melville's Moby-Dick, who is both holy in his whiteness and a sublimely terrifying nothingness. Ahab, the novel's crazed demoniac protagonist, is one of the living dead who regards holiness as evil and finds the very sight of loveliness agonizing. This doomed self-tormentor refuses to give up on his impossible desire for the white whale—a desire which is all that lends him a semblance of life—and, like Heathcliff, pursues this longing all the way into death.

5. I have written on the novel more fully in *The Rape Of Clarissa: Writing, Sexuality and Class Struggle in Samuel Richardson* (Oxford, 1982).

6. (London, 1958).

Index